D1491562

John G. Howieson

The Scots Literary Tradition

THE SCOTS
LITERARY TRADITION

An Essay in Criticism

by

John Speirs

FABER AND FABER

24 Russell Square

London

First published in 1940 *by*
Chatto & Windus
This revised second edition
first published in mcmlxii
by Faber and Faber Limited
*24 Russell Square, London, W.C.*1
Printed in Great Britain by
Western Printing Services Ltd., Bristol

TO RUTH AND LOGAN

Acknowledgements

(1940)

To the Editors of *Scrutiny* for having from time to time published parts of what was to be this book, and especially to Mr. and Mrs. F. R. Leavis for their encouragement and criticism. Also to the Editors of *The Aberdeen University Review* in whose pages there appeared what was to be the chapter on Gavin Douglas's *Aeneid*.

(1962)

Some of the material now included in Part Three has appeared before: "Tradition and Robert Fergusson" in *Robert Fergusson* (Nelson), "Burns' 'To a Louse' and 'Holy Willie's Prayer' " in the Pelican *Guide to English Literature Vol. IV*, and "Burns's Epistles" (B.B.C. Third Programme). For permission to use this material here I am indebted to Nelson & Sons, Penguin Books, B.B.C. and, again, *Scrutiny*. The years have made me only the more conscious of my indebtedness—and that of my generation—to F.R.L.

Contents

Additional Essays

Preface to Edition of 1962

The *Scots Literary Tradition*, as first published in 1940, consisted of Parts One and Two of the present volume. It was written by a young man, and it has seemed unwise for me to attempt to rewrite it now. I have, therefore, allowed Parts One and Two to stand in this new edition much as they were, except for some corrections and interpolations. But there are a few larger additions—including a new essay on Gavin Douglas' *Aeneid*—and I have thought it best to keep these separate from the original book by putting them into an additional section at the end of the present volume.

In its original form, *The Scots Literary Tradition* was written —as articles and reviews—for *Scrutiny* in the thirties, and it belonged in that context. It had its small place in the whole effort at disengagement from what had come to seem limiting nineteenth-century conceptions of poetry (though these were still academic orthodoxy). It began from the recognition that the poetry in Scots, the poetry of Dunbar, Henryson, and Burns, was not congruous with nineteenth-century conceptions of poetry. The re-reading of the Scots poetry could, therefore, assist the whole movement towards a less limited contemporary taste in literature. It may be that, because of this corrective intention, the book emphasized the characteristics of the Scots poetry that were different from those of Romantic or late nineteenth-century poetry. If I were writing the book now I might be less concerned to help to define the limitations of nineteenth-century poetry and rather more concerned to define the limitations of the Scots poetry. But the central conviction in the book stands: that the Scots poetry could and should be enjoyed for the kind of thing it is in itself apart from nineteenth-century ideas of what poetry is, and apart from nineteenth-century English poetry.

But, further, the fact that the book took shape in the context of *Scrutiny* means that it shared the concern for standards and the function of criticism out of which *Scrutiny* itself arose. Contemporary Scotland was viewed for the purposes of the book as being part of the modern world. The provocativeness of what was regarded, at the time, as the pessimism of the book's conclusion was deliberate.

II

This deliberate provocativeness may have done some good, as it was intended to do. It lent a further impetus, as far as could be judged, to the effort towards a modern Scottish consciousness initiated and represented by Hugh McDiarmid (C. M. Grieve), the outstanding personality of our time in Scotland. His work should be considered as a whole and is inseparable from his personality. His prose polemics are as much part of his work of promoting consciousness in Scotland as his verse. His earlier verse—*A Drunk Man Looks at the Thistle* (in Scots) and the *Second Hymn to Lenin* volume (in the English of a Scotsman)—more often hits the mark than, on the whole, his later verse. By comparison, this is often diffuse, rhythmically flat and monotonous. It keeps on making pronouncements about things rather than becoming, as poetry, a crystallization of human experience in all its fulness and diversity. The impression is one of verbosity rather than of complex life. His later argumentative prose, on the other hand, continues still to have the power to seize and hold our interest; it has an inner fire and a fighting force, the prose of a man with strong convictions and something to fight for and against. He still stands for health and life and sincerity in Scotland against complacency and indifference.

The sustained attempt by a number of younger men, inspired by McDiarmid's work, to create a modern poetry in Scots has involved them in attempting to recreate a Scots language in which such a poetry might be composed. The attempt has been given urgency by the recognition that the abandonment of verse composition in Scots would mean acquiescence in the extinction of a national consciousness. The fact had to be accepted that the old Scottish community implied in the poetry of Fergusson and Burns no longer existed. But might there not, it was asked, be a poetry in Scots expressing, indeed creating a modern Scottish consciousness? But a language consciously constructed or reconstructed by a few literary men, even though they may be potentially poets, out of earlier texts (however much loved) or by collecting words and idioms still in use in different parts of the country, or with the aid of national or dialect dictionaries, is not in any real sense a language. It is not the language that is spoken by themselves and the people around them, shaped by the experience of generations and out of which literature has been and can still be made. There can be no modern Scots literature if there is no modern Scots spoken language. The poetry in this consciously constructed Scots suffers, it seems to me, the disabilities of poetry composed in a poetic diction. The words —often archaisms or dialect words nostalgically relished—come between the reader and the experience; they draw attention to themselves away from their object.

This preoccupation with words for their own sake, this attitude to language as an instrument manipulated from the outside has been exacerbated, I think, by the influence of Joyce. It began, at least in some of its modern manifestations, with Flaubert and it led Joyce himself in the end, logically, inevitably to the incredibly skilful and complicated failure of *Finnegans Wake*—a failure of communication. *Finnegans Wake* has to be unmade by the reader before its meaning can become clear, and in being thus unmade it loses any immediacy of effect. Poetry in consciously constructed Scots runs, it seems to me, the same risk. The secret of good writing, as used to be said, and as it would be well to remember, is to have something to say. To the writer composing under the compulsion of experience, the only thing that matters is finding the exact verbal equivalent of that experience—in that sense, finding 'the best words in the best order'. What he has to say imposes its inner discipline of selection and arrangement, and evolves its own rhythm.

At the present time of perplexity about language in Scotland the distinction between the modern poet in Scots and the modern Scottish poet could perhaps be useful. The latter might be the better poet and also be properly described as a Scottish poet. There is, after all, the analogy of Yeats and also of Classic American Literature (as Lawrence called it) in English and yet American. There equally well could be, on that analogy, a modern Scottish literature; and it could be nearer the true expression of a modern Scotsman than poetry in a largely archaic reconstructed Scots. It requires also to be said, perhaps, that there is no need for a modern Scottish author to endeavour to exclude from himself the best that is thought and said outside Scotland; he need not endeavour to be insular; in becoming conscious of the differences between himself and authors of other nationalities he could become the more consciously himself.

Since *A Drunk Man Looks at the Thistle*, there is one notable piece in Scots in which a poet's intensity of personal experience, in his contemporary Edinburgh, has forced itself through the Joycean preoccupation with words, much as in *Ulysses* Joyce's experience of Dublin itself—and its overheard voices —does. In Sidney Goodsir Smith's sequence, *Under the Eildon Tree*, the poet's necessary concern with language and technique, to put it less provocatively, has become to some extent subordinated to his interest in human experience. In No. XIII, in particular, Edinburgh at night—the nightmare modern city of Dickens, Dostoyevsky, Baudelaire—seems to expand fantastically in the drunken consciousness and take on a universal quality like Hell; then again, under the moon, its squalor is enchanted away. Intimations of childlike innocence about the girl, in contrast to her Edinburgh slum environment,

16

end in a fuller recognition of her value as a human person. In another poem of the sequence (No. VI) public men, men of power and worldly ambitions—

> Aa the great michtie
> In their great seats are warslan
> For anither cushion maybe
> Or mair licht
> Or the table
> A wee thing nearer til the great hand

—are weighed in the balance with a 'lassie's fykes' and (as in Propertius) found no weightier.

Another small volume of verse stands out among those published since 1940 in Scotland, George Bruce's *Sea Talk*. These poems are not in Scots and yet they are not English poetry; they could not be more distinctively Scottish. They are the way a particular Scotsman talks, individually so, the talk of one born and bred a Scotsman of a particular locality, the North East seaboard. They are an achieved example of what I had in mind when I spoke of a poetry that could be nearer the true expression of a modern Scotsman than poetry in a reconstructed Scots. If there is any noticeable influence, it is that of *Hugh Selwyn Mauberley* on the expression, which is distinguished by a bareness, an asceticism, a tautness and tenseness of diction and rhythm. But the communicated experience is quite different from Pound.

THE CURTAIN

> Half way up the stairs
> Is the tall curtain.
> We noticed it there
> After the unfinished tale.
>
> My father came home,
> His clothes sea-wet,
> His breath cold.
> He said a boat had gone.

B   17

He held a lantern.
The mist moved in,
Rested on the stone step
And hung above the floor.

I remembered
The blue glint
Of the herring scales
Fixed in the mat,

And also a foolish crab
That held his own pincers fast.
We called him
Old Iron-clad.

I smelt again
The kippers cooked in oak ash.
That helped me to forget
The tall curtain.

Partly, the poignancy of these poems comes from a sense that this recollected world, the world of the North East fishing community with its traditional way of life, has vanished with childhood and boyhood; partly, that it existed not only on the bleak edge of the northern sea but on the edge of the modern World, balanced precariously against chaos and change. These intense personal feelings for what has gone—for particular persons of strong and fine character, persons of the same blood and family, more especially, who have gone—are involved in the poetry with a reaching-out towards permanent and universal truth, 'the stability of truth', in Johnson's phrase.

III

The Scots Literary Tradition was given that title because it was concerned with the tradition of literature in Scots. That accounts for several of what were regarded, at the time, as its omissions. But it does not account for the inclusion of *The House with the Green Shutters*, which is not in Scots (except for the dialogues). The inconsistency of including my review of the World's Classics edition of that novel was nevertheless deliberate. It was not simply that I was anxious to take the

18

chance—even committing an inconsistency by doing so—of commending the most outstanding late nineteenth-century Scottish novel at a time when Stevenson (not to speak of Barrie and John Buchan) continued to be overestimated as representing 'the line of Scott' with the added attraction of 'style'. I wanted to include a book to represent nineteenth-century Scotland—or, more specifically, to indicate some of the things that may have gone wrong with nineteenth-century Scotland and that might explain why it did not achieve a literature. No doubt *The House with the Green Shutters* is one-sided and bitter, a radical book, but useful as an exposure of inhumane aspects of nineteenth-century Scottish life.

The inconsistency of including *The House with the Green Shutters* made, of course, more glaring the apparent injustice of my omission of Scott. Though Scott's work is mostly not in Scots (except for some of the dialogues in the novels and one or two songs and ballads) he could by a similar calculated inconsistency have been included. He was a great Scotsman and Scottish man of letters, and he achieved European fame and influence—comparable only to that achieved, as a philosopher, by David Hume, in his more distinguished eighteenth-century prose. My omission of Scott was, however, deliberate for another reason than that his work does not strictly belong in the context of the literature in Scots which was the subject of the book. The nineteenth-century overestimation of Scott as a novelist was still being heavily endorsed academically. There were extravagant Scott centenary tributes by professors and 'middle-brow' novelists. I could not, for the sake of avoiding giving offence, have countenanced these opinions, even if they were sincerely held. In that context, therefore, my omission of Scott was a deliberate critical act. (I may, perhaps, now add that I had myself gone through a Scott and Stevenson phase in my boyhood and had fully known their appeal. But when I had read more widely I had discovered, to my distress, that the Waverley Novels did not stand the test of the great English, French and Russian novelists of the nineteenth century.)

Scott's novels about the Scotland of the eighteenth and seventeenth centuries are the ones which have permanent value, at least as a record of that Scotland. In these novels Scott is writing about the Scotland of the recent past that had not yet wholly passed away, the traditional Scottish life and manners that he had known from childhood and that he cherished. He writes out of a deep regard for the customary, the long-established, the traditional, a 'piety' as well as an intense antiquarian curiosity about his country's past, the evidences of which he found everywhere around him. This does not quite make him a novelist. He had not, to a high degree, the creative novelist's gift. He had no profound psychological or moral insight—as distinct from an interest in manners and customs and 'sense of the past' in his own locality and country—and not sufficient energy of dramatic presentation of characters and situations to be a great novelist. His Scots dialogues and 'Wandering Willie's Tale' are the parts of his novels which have most life. His eighteenth-century prose has nothing of the distinction of Johnson's great prose or even of that of lesser eighteenth-century masters, and it seems old-fashioned and often incongruous with the subject matter; in his descriptions of action he is like a big man charging up a hillside impeded by a heavy overcoat—but a big man for all that. Scott has, of course, many other claims to our regard besides that of novelist and poet. His work belongs to the history of the development of the historical sense, and he is one of the pioneering medievalists and folklorists.

There is a parallel between Scott's 'sense of the past' (and of 'the spirit of place') and Hawthorne's. But it is exactly when we compare the two that Hawthorne is seen to be the more sensitive and profound as a creative poet-novelist.[1] Hawthorne was intensely preoccupied with seventeenth- and eighteenth-century Puritan New England because he recognized

[1] Hawthorne has attracted a remarkable amount of the best critical attention—by James, Leslie Stephen, Lawrence and, more recently, by Yvor Winters, Marius Bewley and Q. D. Leavis, to all of whom I am indebted.

that it had made his contemporary nineteenth-century New England what it was, and that it might help him to account for the being he himself was and for his personal perplexities. His exploration into that particular past is an exploration into himself; to understand himself in his New England, he had to work back into that past. It is, perhaps, because Scott is not introspective and subjective in this way that his interest in the manners and customs of his people is more simple and less psychological and moral. Hawthorne's imaginative world is much more shadowy and ghostly—though related to objective historical and observed contemporary fact—but finer, more delicately sensitive. It is haunted by the grim New England past, by a sense of the guilt of Puritan ancestors. This is Hawthorne's particular version of 'original sin'. The past was such that he felt it had to be expiated. Puritanism and its theological dogmatism and grim moral code no longer held, but they had left permanent effects, a desiccation, a thinness of life. Not all the effects of Puritanism need have given Hawthorne cause for melancholy. His own sensitive conscience and fineness of taste are, perhaps, themselves among the effects of the Puritan tradition. 'The Puritan conscience', indeed, persists in the New England character at its best throughout the nineteenth century to the time of Henry James as a moral seriousness, a sensitive concern to do the right thing, make the right choice, feel in the right way. It persists also, transmuted, as the earnest, conscientious nineteenth-century New England 'cultivation of taste' (as well as of mere genteelness). But what weighed down and made Hawthorne's gentle spirit more melancholy was the evidence of inhumanity in the Puritan past, the crimes committed, the fanatical repressiveness. He feels as if, as a fated consequence, the land and people were blighted by a curse. But Hawthorne's instinct for life is strong; he experiences an acute sense of deprivation, of being cut off from the fulness of life by the shadow of that past as it seems to him to fall over the landscapes and townscapes of his New England. Scott is so much more comfortable. His Scotland, despite its tragic past, its schisms and divisions, its Calvinist and anti-Calvinist fanaticism and bloodshed, is more comfortable, full of sensible folk and good neighbours, after all, who help to sustain a sense of a long-established, customary, settled way of life, a basic stability and continuity.

The link between Scott and Hawthorne (for the reader, I mean) is James Hogg's *Confessions of a Justified Sinner*. This is a book I should certainly have included if my subject had not been Scots but Scottish literature. Hogg is nearer Hawthorne than Scott in that his exploration into the Calvinist Scottish past is an exploration into himself. It is in fact the psychology to be found in the book that makes it notable, and not the supernaturalism as such (which is that of folk belief and the traditional Scottish tales about the Devil as well as that of the Gothicism of the period). More especially it is the passages in which the supernaturalism is analysable as having a psychological basis.

> We parted with expressions of mutual regret, and when I left him I felt a deliverance, but at the same time a certain consciousness that I was not thus to get free of him, but that he was like to be an acquaintance that was to stick to me for good or for evil. I was astonished at his acuteness and knowledge about everything; but, as for his likeness to me, that was quite unaccountable. He was the same person in every respect, but yet he was not always so; for I observed several times, when we were speaking of certain divines and their tenets, that his face assumed something of the appearance of theirs; and it struck me that, by setting his features to the mould of other people's, he entered at once into their conceptions and feelings . . .
>
> From this time forth I began to be sick at times of my existence. I had heart-burnings, longings, and yearnings that would not be satisfied; and I seemed hardly to be an accountable creature; being thus in the habit of executing transactions of the utmost moment without being sensible that I did them. I was a being incomprehensible to myself. Either I had a second self . . .
>
> The worst thing of all was what hitherto I had never felt, and, as yet, durst not confess to myself, that the presence of my illustrious and devoted friend was becoming irksome to me. When I was by myself, I breathed freer, and my step was lighter; but, when he approached, a pang went to my heart, and, in his

22

company, I moved and acted as if under a load that I could
hardly endure . . .

At the extremity of the Colwan wood, I perceived a figure
approaching me with slow and dignified motion. The moment
that I beheld it, my whole frame received a shock as if the ground
on which I walked had sunk suddenly below me. Yet, at that
moment, I knew not who it was; it was the air and motion of
someone that I dreaded, and from whom I would gladly have
escaped; but this I even had not power to attempt. It came
slowly onward, and I advanced as slowly to meet it. . . .

On the other hand, the world of Hogg is not so rarefied as
Hawthorne's. The shrewd, sensible Scottish humour of certain
of the subsidiary characters is something Hogg's Scotland has
in common with Sir Walter Scott's. Like Mrs. Dean in *Wuthering Heights*, though with less of her homely wisdom, these
characters represent common sense in the presence of irrationality.

IV

If my subject had not been restricted to literature in Scots,
I might have included, in addition to Sir Walter Scott, a
chapter on the Scottishness of Byron in his final comic and
satiric poetry. If Burns had a successor, it was the Byron of
Beppo, A Vision of Judgment, and *Don Juan.*[1] The circumstances and social worlds of the two men could not have been
more different (if indeed Byron could be said ever to have really
belonged to a social world—his experience of the fashionable
Regency world only made him more insistently for a time a
rebel and individualist). Byron had had his day and his fling
as a Regency Milord in that fashionable London world and
could finally, in Italy, look back on it with a disenchanted air,
as a cosmopolitan man of the greater world; Burns belonged
wholly to his own local world (except for his brief lionizing by the
fashionable and cultivated Edinburgh society); and yet there
are essential resemblances between the verse of *Don Juan* and

[1] Though *Don Juan* had little effect on English literature it had much
to do with Pushkin's *Evgeny Onegin*, the poem which inaugurated 'the
great tradition' of the Russian novel.

Burns' Kilmarnock poems. Both poets have more in common with each other than either has with Pope and the Augustan line. A recklessness, a defiance, a gaiety, a kicking over the traces, a devil-may-care spirit, an indecorousness is common to both; Byron had not only English respectability to break away from but also, like Burns, Scottish Calvinism. The air of gay improvization of the verse of *Don Juan*, as if talking at ease among men friends in a convivial hour over a bottle, the apparently slapdash verse (really extraordinarily skilled), the madcap rhyming recall Burns' comic and satiric verse. Both poets have an independent spirit—with a touch of aristocratic insolence and a lighthearted tone of cynicism in Byron's case —a contempt for forms and conventions and class distinctions. Both find a solid basis of value in the idea of a common humanity; the satiric spirit in both is tempered by a warm-hearted geniality and generosity; both assert that what matters is a man's intrinsic worth.

V

A full description of the Scots poetry of the sixteenth century, and of what happened to poetry in Scotland in the seventeenth century, would now have to take account of the work being done by Mrs. Helena M. Shire and her associates. Mrs. Shire is, for instance, investigating the effects of the French connection at the Scottish Court. Comparisons between the Scots and the French, as well as the English, poetry of the period, could result in a new view of the Scots poetry. A regional survey of music commonplace-books kept by certain Scottish families in the seventeenth century has been inaugurated by Mrs. Shire, and she has established the fact that courtly song and court poetry continued to be cherished in certain great households in Scotland well into the seventeenth century long after the Court had left.[1]

[1] In the meantime notice may be drawn to 'Music of Scotland 1500–1700 (*Musica Britannica XV*), edited by Kenneth Elliott and Helena Mennie Shire (London, 1957).

The Scots Literary Tradition was not intended to be a literary history but to be criticisms of poems in Scots—poems viewed for the most part in their chronological order—from which indeed a literary history of Scots poetry might incidentally begin to be seen to take shape. Thus, for my chapter on 'Sixteenth-century Scots Poems' I selected one or two of the poems which I judged to be the *best* poems among those that were known. It has seemed to me that what I wrote about these particular poems may be allowed to stand without much modification. These criticisms could, perhaps should, be expanded by criticisms of any new poems of outstanding merit that have been discovered since or may yet be discovered. The whole pattern formed by the sixteenth-century Scots poetry which we know is always liable to be altered by the discovery of poems of merit.

Introduction 1940

This book is an attempt to focus as a whole and with regard to its bearing on our present problems (as far as that may be possible without distortion) the literary tradition in Scots. This has necessarily tended to give the book in its implicit (and occasionally explicit) application a sociological bias.[1] But I have tried to bear in mind that 'sociological' criticism, as much as 'psychological' criticism, is a deflection from strict 'literary' criticism; and that criticism of literature —to be itself and not another thing—must remain 'literary' criticism.

It has seemed for long urgent that the cultivated, whether Scottish or English, should become more sufficiently cognisant of this tradition as being a whole and as being something distinct from the southern. Realized as such, its powers might have a chance to become effective both as an enrichment and as a corrective.

For a Scotsman to become fully aware of himself it would seem even necessary that he should realize his Scottish past as something at least partially distinct from an English past. For an Englishman perplexed by a sense of exhaustion, in some of its directions, of the English language and tradition it might even be to a limited, but not unimportant, extent revitalizing to grow aware also of the Scots and its resources. A fresh realization, involving a fresh revaluation, of Scots poetry might at the very least help to correct the tendency to narrow

[1] An interest in 'literature and society' is what I meant (1961).

conceptions of what poetry is, such as have from time to time since the seventeenth century damaged English poetry. In general it may perhaps be taken as axiomatic that we cannot be enough conscious at a time such as the present (when they are threatened with neglect and final extinction) of the traditions upon which our intellectual and spiritual life has depended.

PART ONE

1

Fifteenth-century Scots Poetry

The assumption to start from is that the Scots poetry of the fifteenth century really matters to us only when we feel in reading it that it is something as immediate to us as the work of any modern. But to feel it as so immediate is to feel it as what it is, and that is medieval poetry; it is different in important respects from modern poetry. To enjoy it, any more than to enjoy any kind of poetry, we cannot be passive. There must be some effort on our part to stand outside the changes that with time have taken place in that most important part of our mind which is part of the European mind. We cannot know whether the effort is worth making till we have made it. But the study of poetry is a means to enlarging the scope and correcting the balance of our sympathies. The study of medieval poetry may help, in particular, to correct the balance in important respects in which the exclusive study of later poetry will not help.[1]

The Scots poetry of the fifteenth, and of the beginning of the sixteenth, century is still medieval. It has much in common with other medieval poetry in other European languages. This is perhaps the most important fact not only about the Scots poetry but also about the Scotland of the fifteenth century. Europe had a general life, and neither Scotland nor its

[1] To take a literary instance: if we came to Shakespeare from as frequent reading of the medieval poets as we generally do from the reading of the poets since his time, our appreciation of his work might in some respects be different and, perhaps, juster.

poetry was separate from it. The poetry is early (and, as I hope may appear, the most complete and valuable) Scots poetry, and, at the same time, a late development of medieval European poetry.

This poetry has had little critical attention. The direction the criticism of it seems to have taken has been towards establishing Chaucer as its sole fountain-head. This seems to me at once an over-simplification. The extraordinary variety in Chaucer will not account for the extraordinary variety of fifteenth-century Scots poetry. It is as independent of Chaucer as was possible for it to be, allowing for the fact that it also is medieval and that Chaucer was its immediate predecessor. As time went on the separation became greater. There are degrees of separateness from Chaucer in fifteenth-century Scots poetry.

2

The 'Kingis Quair'

The *Kingis Quair* is the medieval Scots poem which is nearest, not merely in the time of its production, but perhaps in itself, to some of the poems of Chaucer.[1] Exactly how far the poem is derivative from them is not so easily determined as may at first seem. Chaucer and the poet of the *Kingis Quair* had something in common which they shared also with other medieval poets. It was not merely that they read and learned from the same poems. Their habit of mind was medieval. It was a habit of mind for which allegory was the normal expression. Our difficulty is to enter into this habit of mind and to understand and appreciate allegorical poetry. The central medieval poetry is allegorical, which is not the same as saying that the best of the Scots medieval poetry (which is very late medieval poetry) is the allegorical; there are reasons for saying it is not; but unless it is possible for us to appreciate the allegorical poetry it must remain doubtful whether we really appreciate the other exactly in the right way.

The *Kingis Quair* cannot be dismissed as a mere conventional exercise in the courtly manner of Chaucer. The following passage, which is remarkably similar to a passage in the *Parlement of Foules* (183–203), may help to illustrate some of the ways in which it is equally alive.

---

[1] It may properly be called Chaucerian, but in a limited sense. It is full of echoes and reminiscences of Chaucer's more medieval poems. The qualities of the greater Chaucer, the poet of the human comedy, are absent.

Quhare, in a lusty plane, tuke I my way,
    Endlang a ryver, plesant to behold,
Enbroudin all with fresche flouris gay,
    Quhare, throu the gravel, bryght as ony gold,
    The cristall water ran so clere and cold,
That in myn ere maid contynualy
A maner soun, mellit with armony;

That full of lytill fischis by the brym,
    Now here, now there, with bakkis blewe as lede,
Lap and playit, and in a rout can swym
    So prattily, and dressit tham to sprede
    Thair curall fynnis, as the ruby rede,
That in the sonne on thair scalis bryght
As gesserant[1] ay glitterit in my sight:

And by this ilke ryversyde alawe
    Ane hye way fand I like to bene,
On quhich, on every syde, a long rawe
    Of treis saw I, full of levis grene,
    That full of fruyte delitable were to sene,
And also, as it come unto my mind,
Off bestis sawe I mony divers kynd:

The landscape is a mythological landscape: it is not merely
decorative. The 'lusty plane', the 'ryver', the 'hyë-way', the
'treis full of fruyte delitable' (reminiscent of the Garden of
Eden) are mythological. They belong to that garden which is
in the centre of medieval poetry, and which, if we think of the
diversity of bird, beast and fish in it rather, perhaps, than the
personifications and gods and goddesses who are also important, is partly the garden of 'kinde'. Bird, beast and fish in it
symbolize that intuition of the unity of all kinds of being
which seems to have been very strongly present to the medieval mind but which we have partly lost. In itself it is perhaps
pagan, though, of course, it is not necessarily incongruous
with the Christianity of the Middle Ages, in that a Christian
poet could easily find a place for the garden and all the bird,
beast and fish in it in some hierarchy of God's created being.

[1] scale-armour.

There is no suggestion in the passage of any conflict between what it represents and something outside it.

The clarity and definiteness of the images ('gravel bryght as ony gold', 'cristall water',[1] 'bakkis blewe as lede', and in a later passage, 'turtur quhite as calk') is very notable, perhaps because they strictly serve the purpose of a meaning outside themselves and yet paradoxically an inner meaning; they have none of the externality of the images in the later more simply—yet more elaborately—'pictorial' allegorical poetry in which if there is a meaning it has got separated from the imagery to the disadvantage of both. To put it another way, the imagery here has not yet begun to develop independently of the meaning into a rhetorical life of its own.[2]

The same cannot be said of the passage in the *Kingis Quair* descriptive of the lady. There is more life in the garden than in her; she is less deeply felt than the leafage of the trees. There is a significant difference also between her and her counterpart, the Emelye of the *Knightes Tale*. Emelye springs into life in the same breath with 'the lilie upon his stalke grene', with 'the rose colour', with 'the sonne up-riste'. She gathers flowers

> To make a sotil gerland for her hede.

Thus, while the description is strictly conventional, it gives that impression of freshness, naturalness and simplicity which is so often noted. But the lady of the *Kingis Quair* is dissociated from the garden, and, in the description of her, jewels are substituted for flowers. The 'plumys' on the lady's head are

[1] Cf. *Roman de la Rose*—Chaucer's translation I. 125, the river
> Tho saugh I wel
> The botme paved everydel
> With gravel ful of stones shene.

[2] There is a philosophic element in the poem, an interplay on the Boethian themes of necessity and free will, fortune and freedom. The man—in contrast to the birds, at whose spontaneous joy he marvels—has not yet experienced love, whose service is freedom, until he looks down from the tower in which he is a prisoner, and for the first times sees his lady in the garden.

said to be like the 'flour jonettis', but they are plumes, not, as in the case of Emelye, flowers. The poet speaks of

> Beautee eneuch to mak a world to dote

but the emphasis is on the lady's 'array', and in that there is a coruscation of jewels. There is very much jewel imagery also in the fourteenth-century *Pearl* (II, stanzas 6–10; IV, stanzas 17–19; XVII, stanzas 83–6) but there it is either in itself symbolical or part of a symbolical landscape; its purpose is to separate, so that there may be no possibility of confusion, the world of the vision from the ordinary world. But in the *Kingis Quair* passage the jewel imagery suggests merely the ornaments of a princess of a court. It is associated, indeed, with fire:

> grete balas[1] lemyng as the fyre . . .
> About her nek, quhite as the fyre amaille[2]
> A gudely cheyne of smale orfeuerye,[3]

from which there hung a ruby

> That as a sperk of lowe[4] so wantounly
> Semyt birnyng upon her quhyte throte,

but in other respects it is without symbolical significance. It produces something of the hard glitter of the later fifteenth-century rhetoric in the gardens of which the flowers have also turned to jewels. The passage is more 'advanced' in a not wholly healthy sense, not only than the Chaucer, but also than the first passage. The decay and death of allegory is implicit in it.

[1] rose-red ruby.   [2] enamel.
[3] goldsmith's work.   [4] flame.

3

Robert Henryson

Chaucer's total achievement, and, to a much lesser extent, probably Dunbar's, exhibits from its beginnings through its maturity to its decay a continuous development, and in this sense is complete. Henryson's, on the other hand, is, though considerable, fragmentary. The *Moral Fables* and the *Testament of Cresseid*, which form the bulk of it, give the impression of being the work of an old man. His total achievement has not (though this does not necessarily follow) the range of Dunbar's, nor, except in the *Testament of Cresseid*, the intensity. It is narrower in this sense without (except in the *Testament*) the compression Dunbar's has.

Not that compression is in itself a test. The complexity of Chaucer's *Troilus*, for example, is not appreciable in a single line, as the complexity of a Shakespeare dramatic poem very often is. It becomes appreciable, because of the diffusion, only after one has been reading for a considerable stretch. Henryson's *Testament* appears to have been done at greater pressure not merely than the rest of his work, which is probably inferior to it, but than Chaucer's *Troilus*, which is superior to it. The two poems are of course totally different, but why the *Testament* is felt to be the less satisfactory, in spite of its pressure, is because it presents a much less complex balance.

Henryson is on the whole more 'popular' than either Chaucer or Dunbar. This is less immediately obvious in the *Testament* than in the *Moral Fables* and certain of the minor poems. The majority of the *Fables* are based on a Latin text of Aesop. But a number are drawn from the popular Reynardian cycle, and a broad folk element is present throughout. The Chaucerian refinement of the verse, French and Italian in origin, is crossed in the *Fables* and in the *Testament* by the native alliterative type (of which the *Sum Practysis of Medecyne* is a superb example).[1] The verse is reinvigorated (as Dunbar's is also) from this source. Certain of the minor poems, on their part, bear an obvious relation to the ballad.

This more 'popular' quality of Henryson is both his strength and his weakness. He is more 'popular' because he is more 'local'. He is further from the European centre than either Chaucer or Dunbar (perhaps partly because he is a 'clerk', not of the court). Yet he is not more Scottish than Dunbar. It is unnecessary to go into the question of national characteristics. The verse of Henryson and Dunbar is Scottish in the first instance because the idiom it is written in is Scottish (or later came to be known as such). Mr. Harvey Wood remarks of this language, 'It is not a spoken, historical dialect of the Scottish language at any period; but an artificial, created "literary" language.' The fact remains that this 'literary' language was created out of a staple of 'spoken' language. The reason why there can be no 'literary' Scots today is because there is no longer a 'spoken' Scots.

It now remains to reinforce these opinions by an examination of the poems themselves in some detail. Henryson is not of course, so 'local' as Burns, nor would it have been to his advantage in his time; but to be just as 'local' as he is does give him certain advantages. It is already a criticism of the

---

[1] Sevin sobbis of ane selche, the quhidder of ane quhaill,
  The lug of ane lempet is nocht to forsaik,
  The harnis of ane haddok, hakkit or haill,
  With ane bustful of blude of the scho bak,
  With ane brewing caldrun full of hait caill,
  For it wilbe the softar and sweittar of the smak.

'Smak' concentrates the pungent flavour. Cf. 'Make the gruel thick and *slab*'—(*Macbeth*, Act IV, Scene 1). The ingredients of Shakespeare's witches' cauldron are obviously drawn from a similar source in 'folk' speech.

Fables to say that it is from them that these advantages may be most readily illustrated. The following is from the *Swallow and the Other Birds*:

> That samin seasoun, in to ane soft morning,
> Rycht blyth that bitter blastis wer ago,
> Unto the wod, to se the flouris spring,
> And heir the Mavis sing and birdis mo,
> I passit ffurth, syne lukit to and ffro,
> To se the Soill that wes richt sessonabill,
> Sappie, and to resave all seidis abill.
>
> Moving thusgait, grit myrth I tuke in mynd,
> Off lauboraris to se the besines,
> Sum makand dyke, and sum the pleuch can wynd,
> Sum sawand seidis fast ffrome place to place,
> The Harrowis hoppand in the saweris trace:
> It wes grit Joy to him that luifit corne,
> To se thame laubour, baith at evin and morne.

There is substance in the joy; it springs from the poet's feeling for the 'business' of the 'labouraris', the 'harrowis hoppand' and the soil 'sappie, and to receive all seedis able'. Through his identification with a locality, and the strenuous activity of the labourers therein,[1] the poet secures a fuller and firmer identification with the whole life and labour of the earth, changing with the seasons. It is related to the moral wholesomeness of his work. It may be said to have imparted a wholesomeness to the 'morality' which in a narrower sense he inherited. The passage implies that his background was not simply (as might be inferred from such a poem as the *Abbey Walk*) the late medieval church, but his whole surrounding Scottish countryside and people.

Another way in which the poet's being 'local' was a source of strength may be illustrated from the description of winter

---

[1] Cf. in the same poem (*Fables*, stanza 261):

> The Lint ryipit, the Carll pullit the Lyne,
> Rippillit the bollis, and in beitis set,
> It steipit in the burne, and dryit syne,
> And with ane bittil knokkit it, and bet,
> Syne swingillit weill, and hekkillit in the flet.

immediately preceding the above passage. The poem from which the passages are taken begins on the theme of the Nature of God, passes to the planets in their spheres, all creatures in their degrees—expressive of the medieval poet's inner sense of harmony, a sense omnipresent in Henryson's work—and passes, by an appropriate transition, to the changing seasons, summer followed by autumn. Up to this point what the poet is beginning to present is the processional pageant of the seasons well within the medieval convention. The life in it—

> And Bachus, God off wyne, renewit hes
> The tume Pyipis in Italie and France

—is rather the remote life of Italy and France than Scotland. But with the description of winter there is a distinct change brought about by the sudden assertion of the poet's 'locality'.[1]

> Than flouris fair faidit with froist man fall,
> And birdis blyith changit thair noitis sweit
> In styll murning, neir slane with snaw and sleit.
>
> Thir dalis deip with dubbis[2] drounit is,
> Baith hill and holt heillit[3] with frostis hair;[4]
> And bewis bene laifit bair off blis,
> Be wickit windis off the winter wair.[5]
> All wyld beistis than ffrom the bentis bair
> Drawis ffor dreid unto thair dennis deip,
> Coucheand ffor cauld in coifis[6] thame to keip.

The actuality of this points forward to the Scottish winter of the *Prologue* to Book VII of Douglas's *Aeneid*.

Henryson's command of the 'popular' element in the language is certainly not more remarkable than Dunbar's. The difference may be suggested, rather negatively, by saying that while the 'popular' element is at least as much present in Dunbar's work as in Henryson's, *more* other elements are present in Dunbar's. This leaves Henryson's work as a whole the more 'popular' in character. But I seem in addition to

---

[1] Cf. in the same poem, *Fables*, stanza 262.   [2] puddles.
[3] covered.   [4] hoar.   [5] ? wild.   [6] caves, nooks.

detect a difference in how and why each uses this 'popular'
element in the language. Henryson (I think of the *Fables*) uses
this element quite naturally because of his partial identity in
his work with the peasant people from whose speech it derives.
His use of it is to that extent less 'literary' than Dunbar's,
whose highly conscious feeling for its raciness and vigour leads
him deliberately, if delightedly, to see what he can do with it
for comic and other purposes of his own.

The difference is reflected in the quality of their humour.
Dunbar's humour is of many varieties, so that it is unsafe to
generalize, but it is relatively seldom quite simply 'folk'
humour. Henryson's humour throughout the *Fables* (to the
actual consideration of which I return) is quite simply 'folk'
humour. A fox[1] stretches himself out on the roadway, 'the
white turnit up of his ene', 'his toung out hung'. A cadgar
'comes carpand with capill and with creillis' and finds him to
all appearances dead.

> He lap full lichtlie about him quhair he lay,
> And all the trace he trippit on his tais;
> As he had hard ane pyper play, he gais.
>
> 'Heir lyis the Devyll' (quod he), 'deid in ane dyke.
> Sic ane selcouth[2] saw I not this sevin yeir;
> I trow ye have bene tussillit with sum tyke,
> That garris you ly sa still withouttin steir:
> Schir Foxe, in Faith, ye ar deir welcum heir;
> It is sum wyfis malisone, I trow,
> For pultrie pyking,[3] that lychtit hes on yow.
>
> 'Thair sall na Pedder,[4] for purs, nor yit for gluifis,
> Nor yit ffor poyntis pyke your pellet[5] ffra me;
> I sall off it mak mittennis to my lufis,[6]
> Till hald my handis hait quhair ever I be;
> Till Flanderis sall it never saill the se.'
> With that in hy, he hint[7] him be the heillis,
> And with ane swak he swang him on the creillis.

---

[1] *The Fox, the Wolf, and the Cadgar.*   [2] marvel.   [3] stealing.
[4] pedlar.   [5] pelt.   [6] hands.   [7] caught.

The comic zest of that, the animal high spirits, is inherent in the language. The language shares the delighted physical energy of those whose speech it originally was—'he trippit on his tais; as he had heard ane piper play'—'with ane swak he swang him'. The farcical end of the *Fox and the Wolf* shows the humour again correspondingly broad. The fox has taken a kid, and because it is Lent[1]—

> He dowkit him, and till him can he sayne:
> 'Ga doun, Schir Kid, cum up Schir Salmond agane!'
> Quhill he wes deid; syne to the land him drewch,
> And off that new maid Salmond eit anewch.

When he has eaten his fill he lies on his back

> Straikand his wame aganis the sonis heit,

and himself remarks

> 'Upon this wame set wer ane bolt full meit.'

Thus, when the keeper's arrow unexpectly pins him to the earth, it is something other than simply poetic justice which is satisfied.[2]

Henryson has been commended for his 'humanity'. If the meaning is that it is the human which Henryson sees in the animal it is a just criticism. It is not the otherness of the animals which attracts his attention: it is their human resemb-

---

[1] In *The Fox, the Wolf, and the Cadgar* the fox also explains, it being Lent, 'I can nocht fische, ffor weiting of my feitt.'

[2] Henryson's moral preoccupation does not so much as might be expected interfere with his humorous observation. In the *Two Mice*, for example, it provides little more than shrewd marginal comment: though sometimes it introduces a certain asperity which sounds personal:

> He fand ane Jolie Jasp, richt precious,
> Wes castin furth in sweeping of the hous.
> As Damisellis Wantoun and Insolent,
> That fane wald play, and on the streit be sene,
> To swoping of the hous thay tak na tent,
> Thay cair na thing, swa that the flure be clene.
> *The Cok and the Jasp.*

lances. It does not occur to the medieval poet to see their life as not one with ours.[1]

> The sweit sesoun provokit us to dance.[2]

They are animated by the same instincts as humans. The 'uplandis mous' and the 'burges mous' know each other's voices 'as kinnismen will do, by verray kind'; and when they meet

> . . . grit kyndnes wes schawin thame betwene
> For quhylis thay leuch, and quhylis for joy thay gret
> Quhyles kissit sweit, quhylis in armis plet.

The two mice are surrounded with much domestic detail which is an additional aid to their identification with common humanity. But in the *Two Mice* and in the opening of the *Paddock and the Mous* there is at the same time a delicate appreciation of the littleness of these creatures as such.

> Ane lytill Mous come till ane Reveir syde;
> Scho micht not waid, hir schankis were sa schort,
> Scho culd not swym, scho had na hors to ryde:
> Of verray force behovit hir to byde,
> And to and ffra besyde that Revir deip
> Scho ran, cryand with mony pietuous peip.
>
> 'Help over, help over', this silie Mous can cry,
> 'For Goddis lufe, sum bodie over the brym.'
> With that ane Paddok, in the water by,
> Put up hir heid . . .
> 'Seis thow', quod scho, 'off corne yone Jolie flat,
> Off ryip Aitis, off Barlie, Peis and Quheit?
> I am hungrie, and fane wald be thair at,
> But I am stoppit be this watter greit.'

The 'schort schankis' and the 'pietuous peip' of the distressed creature suggest the mouse characteristics. 'Scho had na hors

---

[1] There is reproduced in Mr. Harvey Wood's edition before me a picture of the moralizing cock from an early edition of the *Fables*. It looks unmistakably human. The artist need not have been endeavouring to interpret Henryson. He probably still shared in the sixteenth century something of that perception of the medieval poet.

[2] *The Lion and the Mouse.*

to ryde' indicates that she is at the same time human as are her kindred 'in armis plet' in the previous passage. (Burns was not the first to have this kind of feeling for mice, though his poem, coming when it did, has perhaps provided the handiest excuse for the sentimentalization of it.) She sees 'the Jolie flat'. But the river provides a gigantic obstacle:

> But I am stoppit be this watter greit.

The 'seliness' and 'brukkilness' of these creatures are at the same time the 'seliness' and 'brukkilness' of humanity. The birds and beasts of the *Fables* retain just sufficient of the bird and beast characteristics to enliven them in their roles in the human tragi-comedy. They are Scottish country-folk talking. The poet shares their shrewd and humorous knowledge of life, particularly of human weaknesses.

Not all of the *Fables* re-do Aesop; some of them (as I have already noted) belong to the Reynard cycle; there is no other version extant of *The Fox, the Wolf, and the Cadgar*. But they belong as a whole to the great 'popular' tradition of medieval Europe. There are places in them (as in the *Prologue to the Lion and the Mouse*) where Henryson is more 'literary' than 'popular'. But in general where, for example, he comes near to Chaucer it is to the 'popular' Chaucer. Some of the beast conversation in the *Trial of the Fox* is obviously from the same source of *fabliau* tradition, as the debate between the birds in the *Parlement of Foules*. The wolf's head is bloody from the mare's kick. The fox answers the Lion King and Judge's question:

> 'My Lord, speir not at me!
> Speir at your Doctour off Divinitie,
> With his reid Cap can tell you weill aneuch,'
> With that the Lyoun, and all the laif thay leuch.

And so to the sudden change of tone in

> Swa come the yow, the Mother of the Lam

—the lamb murdered by the fox.[1] But though there is in the

[1] Henryson's *Fables* reflect the lawless condition of his contemporary Scotland.

poem (stanza 125) a touch of heraldic imagery there is nothing of the pageantry that Chaucer brought from Italian poetry into the *Parlement of Foules* (230–80).

The comparison between the *Cock and the Fox* and Chaucer's version of the same (the *Nonne Preestes Tale*) brings out Henryson's limitations. The conversation between the cock and the fox (*Fables*, stanzas 64–7) and between the cock's three wives Pertok, Sprutok, and Toppok (71–7) are excellent comedy. But the humour is not equal to the sophisticated humour of Chaucer. Henryson does not compass, as Chaucer does, the fulness of burlesque and mock heroic; nor is there the equivalent of Chaucer's appreciation of the comic absurdity of the erudite cock. There are not the varieties of comedy in the *Cock and the Fox* there are in the *Nonne Preestes Tale*. But of course there are many elements, mostly 'popular' elements ('How! berk, Berrie, Bawsie Broun'), in common.

The *Testament of Cresseid* is perhaps less 'popular' than the *Fables*. But neither is it in the same category as Chaucer's *Troilus and Cresseid*. The *Troilus* has been called a novel. There are many elements in it, it is true, which have been present in the novel and absent for long from verse. What therefore particularly interests a modern in the *Troilus* is that here verse is doing not only as much as the prose of a novel, but something more; the conversational intimacy the verse has acquired from French and Italian verse establishes an understanding between poet and reader. They share between them a superior wisdom. The sophistication of the verse because it implies a sophisticated attitude on the part of poet and reader, itself implies a criticism of the love extravagance. From this technical consideration everything else follows. The Pandarus and the Troilus elements in the poem form, by their co-presence there, an implicit criticism the one of the other. The poem probably shocked its first readers, as every really new poem does: Chaucer seems somewhat concerned about this.

Nothing of Henryson's exhibits this profound sophistication. His work is that of a serious good man. Nevertheless, though much lesser than the *Troilus*, the *Testament* is in its own different way a startling emanation of the medieval mind. It has been suggested that it is impossible to overestimate the debt of Henryson to Chaucer. The *Testament* itself suggests that it is possible. Chaucer and Henryson wrote in general in traditions which were common to both; it is therefore not always easy to estimate the indebtedness of the latter to the former. But the *Testament*, besides being unmistakably original, which does not disprove its indebtedness, contains unexpected things if one attempts to read it in relation to Chaucer. Turning from Chaucer's *Troilus and Criseyde* to Henryson's *Testament*, we at once draw breath in a harsher air. The *Testament* is a poem for Lent, the season of repentance, a wintry season in the north. It is a winter night's tale.

The grave, wise attitude represented by the opening passage is that of the whole poem. The tone is a quiet elderly tone. The poet begins by carefully finding his bearings, the season of the year, the positions of the heavenly bodies, Venus in opposition to 'Phoebus, direct descending doun'.

> Schouris of hail can fra the north discend,
> That scantlie fra the cauld I micht defend.

There is again the actuality in the apprehension of the 'cauld' winter season.

> The Northin wind had purifyit the Air
> And sched the mistie cloudis fra the sky,
> The froist freisit, the blastis bitterly
> Fra Pole Artick come quhisling loud and schill,
> And causit me remufe aganis my will.

The wind that has 'purifyit' the air is 'fra Pole Arctic'. But what follows makes it plain that it is more than the cold of winter the poet seeks shelter from. He has 'traisted' that Venus his 'fadit heart of luve she wald mak green'.

> Bot for greit cald as than I lattit[1] was,
> And in my Chalmer to the fyre can pas.

[1] prevented.

46

Thocht lufe be hait, yit in ane man of age
It kendillis nocht sa sone as in youtheid,
Of quhome the blude is flowing in ane rage,
And in the auld the curage doif[1] and deid,
Of quhilk the fyre outward is best remeid;[2]
To help be Phisike quhair that nature faillit
I am expert, for baith I have assailit.

I mend the fyre and beikit[3] me about,
Than tuik ane drink my spreitis to comfort,
And armit me weill fra the cauld thairout:
To cut the winter nicht and mak it schort,
I tuik ane Quair,[4] and left all uther sport,

The humanity of the ageing poet, in this domestic scene, still speaks to us. The 'fire outward' implies the fire inward which is not there. The change from the outer cold to the inner cold—'in ane man of age' love 'kindillis nocht'—and again the change from the lack of the fire in the blood to the 'fire outward' is what enlarges the significance of the whole passage.

The poem does what it does at a considerable pressure. There is not that easy tone of amused observation and at the same time understanding sympathy there is in the *Troilus*. The *Testament* is much more narrowly concentrated than Chaucer's in more than one sense large poem.[5] The moral horror at the 'uncleanness' of the 'fleshly lusts' that have 'changed in filth' Cresseid's 'femininitie' merges into the purely physical horror of the 'uncleanness' of the leprosy that devours her beauty and youth. When the 'Court and Convocation' that inflicts the poetic justice has

Vanischit away, than rais scho up and tuik
Ane poleist glas, and hir schaddow culd luik:
And quhen scho saw hir face sa deformait
Gif scho in hart was wa[6] aneuch God wait.

[1] dull.   [2] remedy.   [3] warmed.   [4] book.
[5] Henryson represents Cresseid as the cast-off mistress of a great lord. There is little of the courtesy of Chaucer here, though Henryson, too, has pity for Cresseid and for her old father, who receives her back with compassion.
[6] woeful.

There is no such grim moment in Chaucer. It is a moment of sudden recognition that the subtle, silent, gradual change from youth to age has, in the case of Cresseid herself, occurred. The leprosy—in the Middle Ages an ever-present threat to the reader as well—enormously intensifies the horror and brings in the idea of pollution. The effect here and in other places is associated with a certain bareness of statement. The statements are often felt to be understatements. When her 'auld' father 'luikit on hir uglye leppir face' there is 'care aneuch betwix thame twane'. The leper can never again belong to the human community, join in the normal social round. Her father 'deliverit hir in at the Spittaill hous'. 'Deliverit' suggests a thing no longer of human worth; the spital house is 'at the tounis end'. It anticipates the hugger-mugger haste of 'syne buryit hir withoutin tarying' and the poignant laconic epitaph which, in sharp contrasts, sums up her life and death:

> Lo fair Ladyis, Crisseid, of Troyis Toun,
> Sumtyme countit the flour of Womanheid,
> Under this stane, lait Lipper, lyis deid.

The poem works by concentration, compression. The tragedy is concentrated in the final meeting between Troilus and Cresseid in which, though, 'not ane ane uther knew'

> . . . with ane blenk it come into his thocht
> That he sumtime hir face befoir had sene.

But in two passages Henryson does allow himself a certain 'literary' expansiveness against which the *moments* of recognition and decisive action stand out the more sharply. The first of these passages is the phantasmagoric pageant of the Ancient Gods. Praying in the Temple of Venus, Cresseid has bitterly accused Cupid and Venus for her unhappy fate. She is rebellious, not as yet recognizing her own fault, her desertion of Troilus. Suddenly a tremendous event seems (in a vision) to occur in the universe; the divinities of the Seven Planets descend to judge Cresseid for her rebellion against what is, in fact, the Nature of Things.

A close comparison between the passage and Chaucer's

description of the Temple of Mars in the *Knightes Tale* (1117–1192) and of Saturn (1598–1611) only emphasizes the difference between the two. The *Knightes Tale* passages (especially 1137–1145) are a poignant series of sharp realizations of the tragedy and horror in the world; which incidentally suggests that the account of Chaucer in general acceptance requires to be considerably stretched. The *Testament* passage exhibits quite another kind of strength. The following is Henryson's Saturn.[1]

> His face (fronsit),[2] his lyre[3] was lyke the Leid,
> His teith chatterit, and cheverit[4] with the Chin,
> His Ene drowpit, how[5] sonkin in his heid,
> Out of his Nois the Meldrop fast can rin,
> With lippis bla and cheikis leine and thin;
> The Iceschoklis that fra his hair doun hang
> Was wonder greit, and as ane speir als lang.
>
> Atouir his belt his lyart[6] lokkis lay
> Felterit[7] unfair, ouirfret with Froistis hoir,
> His garmound and his gyis[8] full gay of gray,
> His widderit weid fra him the wind out woir;[9]
> Ane busteous bow within his hand he boir,
> Under his girdill ane flasche of felloun[10] flanis,[10]
> Fedderit with Ice, and heidit with hailstanis.

The alliterative element, present so strongly in the Henryson and scarcely at all in the Chaucer, helps to give that its thew and sinew. But, perhaps because of that particular kind of robustious toughness, it is without the poignancy of the Chaucer, and is more of a 'literary' *tour de force*. Whereas Henryson pictures the God Mars '*like* to ane boar whetting his tuskis keen', Chaucer sees 'the sowe freten the child right in the cradel'. The passage is an example in Scots of a mode that persists into Sackville's *Induction*.

---

[1] Apart from the Saturn and the Mars, the Venus and the Mercury are perhaps the most interesting. The figure of the physician (here Mercury) seems to have had some enlarged significance for the late medieval imagination.

[2] frounced, wrinkled.	[3] skin, complexion.	[4] shivered
[5] hollow.	[6] grizzled.	[7] matted
[8] dress.	[9] blew out.	[10] deadly arrows

The Complaint of Cresseid, the second of these passages, is a completely medieval 'complaint' on the mutability theme. 'Fairness' is 'bot ane fading flour' and 'all wealth in eird away as wind it weiris'. The much celebrated garden itself

> Quhair thou was wont full merilye in May,
> To walk and tak the dew be it was day
> And heir the Merle and Mawis mony ane,
> With Ladyis fair in Carrolling to gane,

is subject to the law of transience:

> All is decayit, thy weird is welterit so.

From these recollections of her gay and beautiful vanished youth, she is recalled to her present self:

> And for thy bed tak now ane bunche of stro,

which, together with the 'mowlit breid' and the 'cieder sour', brings us up sharp against the actuality of Cresseid's condition. That the 'complaint' is in some measure felt to be itself vanity becomes explicit not only in the words but in the movement of the rebuke of the leper woman who recalls Cresseid to herself.

> And said, 'Quhy spurnis thow aganis the Wall,
> To sla thyself, and mend nathing at all'.

There is nothing for it but the acceptance of fate however hard:

> Ga leir to clap thy Clapper to and fro,
> And leir efter the Law of Leippir Leid.

The reiterated 'clap thy clapper to and fro' expresses the mechanical monotony, the bleak dreary round of a leper's begging existence.

If the *Testament* is less 'popular' than the *Fables*, the *Orpheus and Eurydice* is less 'popular' still. Yet on inspection of the descent of Orpheus in the last-named poem (the rest of the poem is memorable for the elaborately musical Complaint of Orpheus) it becomes plain that if it is less 'popular' than the *Fables*, it is not through any omission of the 'popular' but its absorption into something less simple. The descent of Orpheus already foreshadows Douglas's *Aeneid* as something possible to Middle Scots poetry. It is certain, from his reference to it, that Douglas had read Henryson's poem, but, of course, he need not have; the descent of Aneas was in any case well within his resources as a Middle Scots poet.

The Henryson begins by telling how Orpheus took his way

> To seik his wyfe attour the gravis gray,
> Hungry and cauld, with mony wilsum[1] wone,[2]
> Withouttin gyde, he and his harp allone.

There is the sureness and certainty of the master, the strict economy, the exact proportioning of means to ends. The 'popular' element is represented in the poem by those 'wonders' and 'marvels' which Orpheus is confronted with on his adventurous journey. (We remember the popularity in the Middle Ages of fantastic stories of travel.)[3]

> Than come he till ane ryvir wonder depe
> Our it a brig, and on it sisteris thre.

Orpheus 'playit a joly spring' and the three sisters, Alecto, Megera, and Tisiphone, were subdued. That 'playit a joly spring' again represents the presence of the 'popular' which is here also the 'Scots' element. The incident of Tantalus will illustrate it more fully.

> Syne come he till a wonder grisely flud
> Drubly and deip, and rythly[4] doun can rin,
> Quhair tantelus nakit full thristy stude,
> And yit the wattir yeid aboif his chin;
> quhen he gaipit thair wald no drop cum In;
> quhen he dowkit the watter wald discend;
> Thus gat he nocht his thrist (to slake) no(r) mend.
>
> Befoir his face ane naple hang also,
> fast at his mowth upoun a twynid (threid).
> quhen he gaipit, It rollit to and fro,
> and fled, as it refusit him to feid.

---

[1] wandering.   [2] wan.

[3] Is it an accident that the line

> Fer and full fer and ferrer than I can tell

might be a line from the Ballads?

[4] quickly.

> Than Orpheus had reuth of his grete need
> he tuk his harp and fast on it can clink:
> The wattir stud, and tantalus gat [a] drink.

The rhyme on 'clink . . . drink' (while at the same time em-
phasizing the finality that is characteristic of the whole descent
passage) marks the continued presence of the 'playit a joly
spring' element. The passage is 'Scots' of course in so far as
the language ('gapit', 'duckit', 'rockit') is 'Scots'. The topo-
graphy of Hell is correspondingly related to that of Scotland:

> Syne our a muir, with thornis thick and sharp.

By these means Henryson realizes the Classical theme anew
as a Scots poet; and not without humour, for when Orpheus
remarks that Eurydice is pale, Pluto answers

> She faris as weill daily as does myself,

and adds wisely

> Were she at hame in her countree of Thrace

she would soon be her former self again. But this element does
not subtract from the dignity and impressiveness of the whole.
The enumeration of the past great ones of the Earth whom
Orpheus sees in Hell is not Dante, of course, but is at its level
as medieval. 'There fand he mony careful king and queen' and
'mony paip and cardinal'. At last, after the kings and popes,
he sees Eurydice

> Lene and deidlyk, peteouss paill of hew,
> Rycht warsche[1] and wane,[2] and walluid[3] as the weid
> Her lilly lyre[4] wes lyk unto the leid.

The descent of Orpheus is as a whole a medieval variation on a
Classical theme; and not only medieval but Scots, and not only
Scots but (at least as much as the *Testament*) European; and it
is all these without being any the less one of them and without
being any the less one.

There is nothing of Henryson's with which to compare the
Kingis Quair on the one hand or the *Goldyn Targe* on the other.

[1] sickly.   [2] pallid.   [3] withered.   [4] complexion.

Henryson has no set allegory to correspond with these; which does not mean that there is no allegorical element in his work. This element is sufficiently important in his work, as in the work of all the Middle Scots poets, to justify the keeping of the *Kingis Quair* in mind when reading as an established background against which to set it. Just as the allegorical habit is more alive in some of the poems of Dunbar other than the set allegories, so the allegorical habit is sufficiently alive in Henryson's work. The *Fables* themselves are a kind of allegory, birds and beasts playing humans, although they do not belong to the *Kingis Quair* and *Goldyn Targe* line. Perhaps partly because they do not belong to that line there is scarcely anything in the *Fables*, or anywhere else in Henryson, of that rhetoric which has been observed as beginning even in the *Kingis Quair*, and which the allegories in that line were to develop into. He is almost as free from that as Chaucer himself; and in general he exhibits some of the advantages there may be at certain times in being out of the main stream of change.[1]

[1] Among Henryson's shorter pieces, *The Garmont of Gude Ladies*, a poem with a taking metrical movement, describes the dress he would have his lady wear; she should be dressed in virtues and heavenly graces:

> Hir slevis suld be of esperance,
> To keip hir fra dispair;
> Hir gluvis of gud govirnance
> To gyd hir fyngearis fair.

A charming portrait of a lady is revealed, and here Henryson is a very gentle moralist.

4

William Dunbar

To Dunbar Chaucer has become the 'rose of rethoris all'; the phrase is sufficient to awaken doubt as to the substantiality of Dunbar's appreciation of Chaucer. An examination of his poetry reveals that as a poet he is in fact as different from Chaucer as it was possible for another medieval poet to be. Of course he inherits some of the Chaucerian modes and themes, as he inherits others which, though medieval, are not specifically Chaucerian. But even when Dunbar borrows from Chaucer it is always the differences from Chaucer that are more striking than the resemblances. Plainly, to begin an account of Dunbar from a comparison between his work and that of Chaucer would not be much to the point, unless to bring home the inaccuracy of styling Dunbar a Scottish Chaucerian. He is at a still further remove from Chaucer than Henryson, and, perhaps because he was 'a court man', being nearer the European centre in his time than the latter, he belongs to the very latest medieval phase.

But to find the explanation of Dunbar's power in the influence, already, of the Renaissance would, again, be a misrepresentation. What gives him (in spite of, and because of, his 'lateness') his extraordinary power, whereby he is perhaps the greatest Scottish poet, is his skilled command of the rich and varied resources of language open to him, and, related to this, his command of varied metres adapted from what were by his time the rich accumulations of medieval French and medieval Latin verse, as well as, and often united together

54

with, indigenous alliteration and assonance used as Hopkins rather than as Swinburne uses it. This variety of language and of metres has its counterpart in a variety of modes so bewildering that our first difficulty must be to determine where the centre of Dunbar's work as a whole is. Dunbar's technical skill and versatility are what may first strike the reader. It may be that his poetry appears to be more various than it really is. There is a variety of modes and moods, a vigour and directness, but not a Chaucerian large view of experience. It is my object in this chapter to suggest that the core of his living achievement, that part of his achievement which we read as if it were contemporary, consists, not of the ceremonial poems, *The Goldyn Targe, The Thrissil and the Rois*, but of the comic and satiric poems, *The Twa Mariit Wemen and the Wedo, The Dance of the Sevin Deidly Sinnis*, the goliardic blasphemies, *The Flyting, The Satire on Edinburgh*, and the more acrid and radical satires that merge into the saturnine poems that give his work as a whole, for all its intense vitality, its dark cast.

These comic and satiric poems are not less traditional than the ceremonial poems. The difference is in the nature of their several traditions, or, to put it otherwise, in the ways in which they are traditional; and this again works down to a difference in their language, and social and moral implications of which should appear. The language of the comic and satiric poems is essentially the language of what was living speech in Dunbar's 'locality', which was not without its place in the still homogeneous medieval European community; whereas the 'aureate diction' of the ceremonial poems of Dunbar, the court poet, is at a distinct remove from living speech, and therefore from life, including Dunbar's own, in any locality; is in fact purely 'literary' or 'poetical', rootless, without actuality. The difference between the former and the latter is in consequence that between a greater and a much lesser degree of inherent life. Without life informing it, language, however brilliant its surface, and however aristocratic its lineage, is verbiage.

Yet *The Goldyn Targe* and *The Thrissil and the Rois*, though they may be pressed to one side, for the lively reader, by the vitality of the comic and satiric poems, are what in Dunbar's case had become of the direct line of European allegorical poetry descending from the *Roman de la Rose*, and on this ground they demand some attention in any attempt to give an account of Dunbar's work as a whole. To Dunbar himself and to his contemporaries they doubtless seemed the centre of his work, as indeed they might be if the value of a poem is in proportion to the amount of conscious effort that seems to have been expended on it. But even to Dunbar's first readers I doubt if they were the poems which really yielded the most enjoyment. These heavily ornate poems, with their bejewelled formal landscapes, dazzle the eye; but, except here and there, life has largely escaped from them. There is little that is spontaneous about these show-pieces.

The terms of Dunbar's celebration of Chaucer and Gower at the end of *The Goldyn Targe* are inappropriate in everything else except that they fit their context. It is Dunbar himself in *The Goldyn Targe*, not Chaucer, whose 'termis' are 'enamelit' and 'celicall' and whose 'lippis', 'tonguis', 'mouthis' are 'sugarit', 'aureate', 'mellifluate'. He goes wrong here as a critic, at the same time unconsciously revealing why here he goes wrong also as a poet. The first five stanzas of the poem are a dazzling exercise in the rhetoric, the heavy ornamentation, the overloaded decorativeness, then, in that 'late' century, fashionable. But the poem is inadequate as a poem not because it is rhetoric, but because of the nature of that rhetoric itself. Rhetoric must be something more fundamental, more deeply rooted, than this, to be at the same time fully satsifactory as poetry. Dunbar's highly conscious interest in language carried with it certain obvious dangers. There is a kind of mechanical delight generated in the sheer verbal exercise; but it is not the same thing as the life, the abundant energy of the living language which Dunbar elsewhere successfully shares. *The Goldyn Targe* remains a monument to the fact that a poem cannot be made out of an interest purely in language, and the manipulation and arrangement of it; and when the interest is in 'poetic' language artificially enriched by over-lavish borrowing from alien sources, the resulting kind of richness may easily be fatal to life. Where this kind of rhetoric wears off, as in the beautiful passage about a hundred ladies who land in a meadow from a ship, it is significant that the poetry is revealed as something much more like Spenser than even the Chaucer of the translation of the *Roman de la Rose*. Medieval allegory is here seen changing into something else; it is the death of allegory, its swan-song.

The ceremonial poems were of course written for ceremonial occasions; they correspond to the pageants and processions of these royal and other occasions. To this extent they correspond to something in the public life of Dunbar and the Scotland of Dunbar's time in which ritualistic pomp and show, pageants and processions, played a part such as to suggest, the times being late, that this heightening of the outward forms, this colouring up of the outward shows, is the symptom of some inner spiritual corruption rather than simply what it may at first seem, the spontaneous expression of the natural joy of life in a rather primitive people; there is nothing spontaneous about *The Goldyn Targe*. We cannot afford to ignore this in trying to understand the meaning of Dunbar's work as a whole. Together with the conscious interest in language the ceremonial poems exhibit, it may have a bearing on the other poems of Dunbar that are so unlike the ceremonial poems.

At this point we may well have begun to ask whether Dunbar gained anything by being, in his particular place and time, a court poet. What he did gain may be exemplified most purely by the small poem *To a Ladie*. If the ceremonial poems show that he was among other things a professional court poet, the lyric *To a Ladie* shows him capable also of a genuine courtliness. It would seem absurd to claim uniqueness for this trifle, except in the obvious sense that every poem is unique; but in Dunbar's work it is something of a rarity, something of a surprise in itself; it is at one end of his range; in it the main European tradition is alive, not as in the ceremonial poems dead. Nor is it simply a concentration of what Dunbar does diffusely in the ceremonial poems; it contains something that is not there present; there is in it a certain unexpectedness, almost wit.

> Sweit rois of vertew and of gentilnes
> Delytsum lyllie of everie lustynes.

You would expect 'lily' where you get 'rose', and 'rose' where you get 'lily'; they are interchanged: the lady is virtuous and desirable at the same time. The poem shows Dunbar's skill as a metrist; but that skill is, here, not merely metrical; it is part of the unexpectedness; it contributes, for example, to the surprise of the final line of the first and, again, the second stanza. Allegory and wit are thus brought together, the *Roman de la Rose* and, except that the poem remains in itself completely medieval, the conceitedness of the sixteenth century Petrarchan sonnets. This intellectual element in it, balancing the emotional, is exactly what the purely 'local' love songs of Burns are without.

But, as has been indicated, *To a Ladie* is not representative of Dunbar's characteristic achievement. It is in the comic and satiric poems in colloquial Scots that the sap flows vigorously, that Dunbar's central creative energy finds in various shapes and forms its free and full expression; and it is (I think) in *The Twa Mariit Wemen and the Wedo*[1] that the comic zest, the sheer enjoyment and appetite, reaches its maximum of bursting exuberance; for this poem, though in the tradition of the *chanson à mal mariée* (This is how these women, when they get

---

[1] My account of the poem in *The Age of Chaucer* (1954) is more sober: 'Dunbar's wives are much less complete human beings than the Wife of Bath. In them, human nature is reduced to its animal elements. . . . Outwardly they are noblewomen, splendidly attired, gay court-ladies, but they expose themselves in their private gossip as merciless, primitive creatures, at the level of instinct and appetite. They tear at their men 'with murderous paws'. The poem is strong meat, and presents the brutal obverse side of the poetry of courtly love. The descriptions of the midsummer night, which draw upon the aureate diction and contrast effectively with the colloquial Scots of the monologues, produce an effect of midsummer opulence, rococo June with its festoons of flowers and leaves and its singing birds, and contrast sharply with the horrors exposed.'

together in secret, tear their husbands limb from limb), is
primarily comic, not satiric; in it we devour the ripe grapes.
The force of vulgar gossip is raised to the degree of art;
ribaldry assumes this proportion.

> I wald me prunya[1] plesandly in precius wedis,
> That luffaris myght apone me luke and ying lusty gallandis,
> That I held more in daynte and derer be ful mekill
> Ne him that dressit me so dink;[2] full dotit wes his heyd.
> Quhen he wes heryit[3] out of hand to hie up my honoris,
> And payntit me as pako,[4] proudest of fedderis,
> I him miskennyt, be Crist, and cukkald him maid:

What the poem seems essentially to represent is the force of
the impudent ('lowd thai lewch') natural self rising up from
among the people and asserting its right according to the 'law
of luf, of nature and of kynd' without respect for moral
authority, the dogmas and restraints of the Church.

> Ladyis, this is the legand of my lif, though Latyne it be
> nane.

But the profane figure of the widow in church is an object of
purely comic contemplation; there is no hint of arbitrary con-
demnation.

> Than lay I furght[5] my bright buke one breid one my kne,
> With mony lusty letter ellummynit with gold;
> And drawis my clok forthwart our my face quhit,
> That I may spy, unaspyit, a space me beside: . . .

> Quhen frendis of my husbandis behaldis me one fer,
> I haif a watter spunge for wa, within my wyde clokis,
> Than wring I it full wylely and wetis my chekis,

(The consequence is she is provided with no dearth of lovers in
secret.)

> And all my luffaris lele, my lugeing persewis,
> And fyllis me wyne wantonly with weilfair and joy:
> Sum rownis;[6] and sum ralyeis;[7] and sum redis ballatis;

| [1] preen. | [2] neat. | [3] harried. | [4] peacock. |
| [5] forth. | [6] whispers. | [7] jests. | |

Sum raiffis[1] furght rudly with riatus speche;
Sum plenis;[2] and sum prayis; some prasis mi bewte,
Sum kissis me; sum clappis me; sum kyndnes me proferis;

In spite of the dramatization we to an appreciable extent share, we are made partakers of the comforts of 'these creatures of the kyn of Adam', the stolen delight in unrestrained sin; the eavesdropper behind the hawthorn is scarcely an intruder.

Apon the Midsummer evin, mirriest of nichtis,
I muvit furth allane, neir as midnicht wes past
Besyd ane gudlie grein garth, full of gay flouris,
Hegeit, of ane huge hicht, with hawthorn treis
Quhairon ane bird, on ane bransche so birst out hir notis . . .
I saw thre gay ladeis sit in ane grene arbeir . . .
Thir gay Wiffis maid game amang the grene leiffis;
Thai drank and did away dule[3] under derne bewis;
Thai swapit[4] of the sweit wyne, thai swanquhit[5] of hewis.

There is no essential contrast between the natural scene (described, because background, in more conventional language, but still bursting with the opulence of midsummer) and the gossips; the beauty of nature and the ugilness of vice, as some moralist has suggested. The hawthorn, the birds and the gossips are filled with the same heady wine, the same exuberance of life; they are equally on the plane simply of nature and instinct.

The Dance of the Sevin Deidly Sinnis comes from the same common source in the popular speech, though in another of these traditions, and exhibiting another variety of this humour The humour here is savage, primitive, uncivilized. Its expression is conditioned by the dance frenzy in the rhythm; for the poem is a *dance* of the Sins. It goes to the pipes or fiddle. The caricature figures of the satanic pageant are caught up in the dance which ends in a wild reel of Highlandmen, smothered by the Devil with smoke.

[1] raves.   [2] complains.   [3] sorrow.
[4] quaffed.   [5] swan-white.

And first of all in dance wes Pryd,
With hair wyld bak and bonet on syd,
Lyk to mak waistie wanis;[1]
And round abowt him, as a quheill,
Hang all in rumpillis[2] to the heill
His kethat[3] for the nanis:
Mony prowd trumpour[4] with him trippit,
Throw skaldand fyre ay as thay skippit
Thay gyrnd with hiddous granis.[5]

The poem has been commended for a conscious blending of
the comic with the horrible, the ghastly, the macabre; but that
is to misunderstand the essential nature of this savage folk-
humour. There is no such dichotomy and no such sophistication in this poem. There is no fantasy or supernatural element
in it either. It shares the vigorous, earthy actuality of the
popular sermons of the Middle Ages.

Syne Sweirnes,[6] at the secound bidding,
Come lyk a sow out of a midding,
Full slepy wes his grunyie:[7]
Mony sweir bumbard[8] belly huddroun,[9]
Mony slute[10] daw[11] and slepy duddroun.[12]

Him followit mony fowll drunckart,
With can and collep,[13] cop and quart,
In surffet and exces;
Full mony a waistles[14] wallydrag,[15]
With wamis unweildable, did furth wag.

There is no incongruity, intentional or otherwise, in introducing
the figure of the Highlandman at the end; Pride ('bonnet on
side') and Ire are just as 'local'. But they are at the same time
'local' against the whole medieval religious (and ecclesiastical)
background.

Quhill preistis come in with bair schevin nekkis,
Than all the feyndis lewche and maid gekkis,[16]
Blak Belly and Bawsy Brown.

[1] make houses bare, i.e. waste their substance on clothes.
[2] tails   [3] gown.   [4] deceiver.   [5] groans.   [6] Sloth.
[7] snout.   [8] drone.   [9] glutton.   [10] sluttish.   [11] slattern.
[12] ? sloven.   [13] flagon.   [14] without a waist (i.e. fat).   [15] sloven.
[16] mocking gestures.

The Dance of the Sevin Deidly Sinnis belongs to the grotesquerie of the late medieval popular imagination.

We shall by this time have observed that there is a good deal of the goliard even in those poems of Dunbar which are not, as *The Dregy of Dunbar* and *The Testament of Kennedy* are, primarily goliardic. The goliardic parodies should be read with Dunbar's own serious hymns in mind. These latter are scrupulously on the model of the Latin hymns, ritualistic, formal, stiff. The symbolism (I think of the beautiful 'Rorate celi desuper') is the extremely conventional symbolism of the Latin hymns. Latinized diction is used; and lines of Latin are inserted. But the ecclesiastical world, the language of which was Latin, was something actual in Dunbar's own world; the lines of Latin fit, without incongruity, into even his profane poems, as they would not into the purely 'local' poems of Burns. The incongruity in the goliardic poems is not essentially between the Latin lines and the Scots (most goliardic poems were wholly in Latin), but in the clash between sacred associations and the profane sentiments of lustfulness, eating and drinking.

> Ego pacior in pectore,
>   This night I myght nocht sleip a wink;
> Licet eger in corpore,
>   Yit wald my mouth be wet with drink.
> Nunc condo testamentum meum,
>   I leiff my saull for evermare,
> Per omnipotentem Deum,
>   In to my lordis wyne cellar;
> Semper ibi ad remanendum,
>   Quhill domisday without dissever,
> Bonum vinum ad bibendum,
>   With sueit Cuthbert that luffit me nevir.
> A barell bung ay at my bosum,
>   Of warldis gud I had na mair;
> Corpus meum ebriosum
>   I leif on to the toune of Air.

The blasphemy of the goliardic poems is the complement of the dogmatic belief accepted (there is no reason not to suppose sincerely) in the serious hymns. Dunbar is one of the last of

the goliards, a descendant of the *clerici vagantes* of the earlier
Middle Ages; in many of his lyrics he is more like his near-
contemporary Villon, in this respect, than Chaucer.

Dunbar's satire when it is serious is, as we should expect,
predominantly ecclesiastical and, at its deepest, religious. *The
Satire on Edinburgh* is not satire of this serious kind; it is again
(unless I am much mistaken, for it has been found scathingly
bitter) less satiric than comic.

> May nane pas throw your principall gaittis[1]
> For stink of haddockis and of scattis,
> For cryis of carlingis and debaittis,
> For fensum[2] flyttingis of defame:
>   Think ye not schame,
> Befoir strangeris of all estaittis
> That sic dishonour hurt your name!
>
> Your stinkand Scull, that standis dirk,
> Haldis the lycht fra your parroche kirk;
> Your foirstairis makis your housis mirk,
> Lyk na cuntray bot heir at hame:
>   Think ye not schame,
> Sa litill polesie to wirk
> In hurt and sklander of your name!
>
> At your hie Croce, quhar gold and silk
> Sould be, thair is bot crudis and milk;
> And at your Trone bot cokill and wilk,
> Pansches,[3] pudingis of Jok and Jame:
>   Think ye not schame,
> Sen as the world sayis that ilk
> In hurt and sclander of your name!

Plainly Dunbar is here thoroughly enjoying himself, even if
the enjoyment is subordinated to a fairly serious and respec-
table intention. The poem conveys the character of the town,
its noises and smells, what it was like to live in. The impression
is of a lively place, the habitat of a boisterous and vigorous
community crowded together among high houses that shut out
the sun from one another and from the streets. *The Flyting of*

---

[1] streets.   [2] offensive.   [3] tripe.

Dunbar and Kennedy is a poem of essentially the same nature. The two poets abuse each other like two fishwives, though it is of course a kind of game. It is a comic *tour de force* of sheer language, but because the language is in this case living language, the coarse-textured vigorous language of the actual popular speech, it does not separate the poet from life but carries him towards it, its own life, wild, savage, uncivilized as its humour again is here.

> Thow bringis the Carrik clay to Edinburgh Cors
>   Upoun thy botingis,[1] hobland, hard as horne;
>   Stra wispis hingis owt, quhair that the wattis[2] ar worne;
> Cum thow agane to skar us with thy strais,[3]
>   We sall gar scale[4] our sculis all the to scorne,
> And stane the up the calsay quhair thow gais.
>
> Off Edinburch the boyis as beis owt thrawis,
>   And cryis owt ay, 'Heir cumis our awin queir Clerk!'
> Than fleis thow lyk ane howlat chest with crawis,
>   Quhill all the bichis at thy botingis dois bark,
>   Than carlingis cryis, 'Keip curches[5] in the merk,[6]
> Our gallowis gaipis: lo! quhair ane greceles gais.'
>
> Than rynis thow doun the gait with gild of boyis,
>   And all the toun tykis hingand in thy heilis;
> Of laidis and lownis thair rysis sic ane noyis,
>   Quhill runsyis[7] rynis away with cairt and quheilis,
>   And cager aviris[8] castis bayth coillis and creillis,
> For rerd of the and rattling of thy butis;
>   Fische wyvis cryis, Fy! and castis doun skillis[9] and
>   skeillis,[10]
> Sum claschis the, sum cloddis the on the cutis.[11]

Flyting passages, monstrous pilings-up of language,[12] are a

---

[1] boots.   [2] welts.   [3] straws.   [4] release.   [5] kerchiefs.
[6] mirk.   [7] horses.   [8] cart-horses.   [9] baskets.
[10] pails, basins.   [11] ankles.
[12] Dunbar's vocabulary of scurrility and abuse is remarkable. Cf. from *Complaint to the King*.

> Bot fowll, jow-jowrdane-hedit jevellis,
> Cowkin-kensis, and culroun kevellis;
> Stuffettis, strekouris, and stafische strumellis;

feature of both Dunbar's comic and satiric poems, and serve
their various ends.

But there are many poems, many of them satiric, and together forming a considerable part of Dunbar's poetry, in
which plainly the poet is not enjoying himself, in which he is
something of a malcontent. To these sardonic or morose poems
we must finally turn to complete the meaning of Dunbar. At
the root of these poems is the overpowering feeling that the
times are late and evil everywhere dominant in the world.

> The clerkis takis beneficis with brawlis,
> Some of Sanct Petir, and some of Sanct Pawlis.
> Take he the rentis, no cair hes he
> Suppois the devill tak all thair sawlis.[1]

> Sic pryd with prellatis, so few till preiche and pray;
> Sic hant of harlettis with thame bayth nicht and day.[2]

> Wyld haschbaldis, haggarbaldis, and hummellis;
> Druncartis, dysouris, dyvowris, drevellis,
> Misgydit memberis of the devellis;
> Mismad mandragis off mastis strynd,
> Crawdonis, couhirttis, and theiffis of kynd;
> Blait-mowit bladyeanes with bledder cheikis,
> Club-facet clucanes with clutit breikis,
> Chuff-midding churllis, cumin off cart-fillaris,
> Gryt glaschew-hedit gorge-millaris . . .
> Panting ane prelottis contenance
> Sa far above him set at tabill
> That wont was for to muk the stabell;
> Ane pykthank in a prelottis clais,
> With his wavill feit and wirrok tais,
> With hoppir hippis and henches narrow,
> And bausy handis to beir a barrow; . . .
> With gredy mynd and glaschane gane,
> Mell-hedit lyk ane mortar-stane.

The monstrous exaggeration develops into caricature, as again, for
example, in *A General Satyre*.

> Sic fartingaillis on flaggis als fatt as quhaillis,
> Facit lyk fulis with hattis that littill availlis,
> And sic fowill tailis, to sweip the calsay clene,
> Thet dust upskaillis; sic fillokis with fucksaillis. . . .

[1] *Of Discretion in Taking.*　　　[2] *A General Satyre.*

'This is the end' is the final feeling conveyed. Distrust infects
the air.

> Is na man thair that trestis ane uthir . . .[1]

> Fra everie mouthe fair wordis procedis
> In everie harte deceptioun bredis
> Flattrie weiris ane furrit goun.[2]
> The sugurit mouthis with myndis thairfra
> The figurit speiche with faceis twa . . .[3]

The disillusion is mature and deep-seated; it proceeds from an
ultimate dissatisfaction with everything that was connoted by
the phrase 'the world'.

> . . . the warld, feignid and false,
> With gall in hairt, and honied hals.

I have ventured to call the satire in these poems, directed as
it is chiefly (though by no means wholly) against ecclesiastics,
not merely ecclesiastical but religious (though negatively so)
because of the consciousness in them of the loss or absence of
goodness and of any assurance of spiritual reality. The nearest
Dunbar comes to such an assurance seems to me perhaps to
be here:

> Lord sen in tyme sa sone to cum
> De terra surrecturus sum,
> Rewarde me with na erthlie cure
> Bot me ressave in regnum tuum
> Sen in this warld may non assure.

The question, to what extent the morbidity in these poems was
temperamental, in Dunbar's case, and to what extent it was
imposed on his poetry by his world, need not trouble us. It is
plainly something both profoundly personal and, since it is
common to late medieval poetry, much more than personal.
In the *Meditatioun in Wyntir* it is given unusually *personal*
expression. Winter was no doubt, especially for Dunbar,
wretched enough in itself, but it is explicitly from something

---

[1] *Tydingis fra the Sessioun.*   [2] *Into this World may none Assure.*
[3] *Of the Warldis Instabilitie.*

more even than winter that he turns with such anxiety to the new season.

> For feir of this all day I drowp;
> No gold in kist, nor wyne in cowp,
>   No ladeis bewtie, nor luiffis blys,
>   May lat me to remember this,
> How glaid that ever I dyne or sowp.
>
> Yit, quhone the nycht begynnis to schort,
> It dois my spreit sum pairt confort,
>   Off thocht oppressit with the schowris.
>   Cum, lustie symmer! with thi flowris,
> That I may leif[1] in sum disport.

It is not only winter that oppresses his spirits, but his morbid moods and thick-coming fancies. He turns with anxiety to summer, as he has turned to song, dance, plays, wine, some lady's beauty, to escape from oppressive fears of age and death. This morbidity in fact explains the Epicurean strain in Dunbar's poetry, the desperate grasping at vivid enjoyments and vivid delights; Dunbar's mirth is often of a violent character.

> Now all this tyme lat us be mirry
> And sett nocht by this warld a chirry,
> Now, quhill thair is gude wyne to sell,
> He that dois on dry breid wirry,
> I gif him to the Devill of hell.

The frequent images of dancing, music, drinking of red wine,

> Sangis, ballatis, playis,

symbolize these delights, and the sprightly dance measures of many of his poems express them. But just as frequent is the sinister image of the gallows gaping, the violent images of cut-throats and cut-purses, and 'cartes' and 'dyce' associated with evil. It is here that a comparison with Villon suggests itself. The obsession with death[2] was inevitable to some part of Dunbar's poetry coming where it did; Dunbar inherited a

---

[1] live.

[2] *Of Man's Mortalitie* is one of Dunbar's finest impersonal expressions of it.

WILLIAM DUNBAR

world, sensed as fallen, mouldering in decay. That the sense
of mortality is not more pervasive in his poetry than it is is
due to the force of that tremendous principle of life (represented in *The Twa Mariit Wemen and the Wedo* and the other
primarily comic poems) he could at times share with the
Scottish people. But where there is no assurance of a spiritual
reality behind a clairvoyant recognition of the vanity of
earthly things, the worm of death and corruption finally
devours everything that is,

> Death followis life with gapand mouth
> Devouring fruit and flowering grane.

and the human procession becomes Death's.

> On to the ded gois all Estatis,
> Princis, Prelotis, and Potestatis,
> Baith riche and pur of al degre;
> *Timor mortis conturbat me.*

> He takis the knychtis in to feild,
> Anarmit under helme and scheild;
> Victour he is at all mellie;
> *Timor mortis conturbat me.*

> That strang unmercifull tyrand
> Takis, on the moderis breist sowkand,
> The bab full of benignite;
> *Timor mortis conturbat me.*

> He takis the campion in the stour,[1]
> The capitane closit in the tour,
> The lady in bour full of bewte;
> *Timor mortis conturbat me.*

The Latin phrase lends a liturgical solemnity to the contrasting
familiar Scots, like a funeral bell tolling. But what makes
Dunbar's poem speak directly to us is its homely personal
note—the makar's concern about his friends and, finally, himself as subject to the inevitable common fate.

> The flesche is brukle, the Fend is sle;
> Timor Mortis conturbat me.

[1] battle.

5

Gavin Douglas's 'Aeneid'

Although Douglas's *Aeneid* would not have existed as what it is but for Virgil's *Aeneid*, its poetic value consists in its present independent existence as a poem of a different language and tradition from the poem of which it is a translation. If we read Douglas's *Aeneid* as Douglas's translation of Virgil's *Aeneid*, our attention will be distracted between two poems, and our enjoyment of the one interfered with by a sense of its failing to be the other. Ezra Pound has remarked that Douglas's *Aeneid* is a better poem than Virgil's. Whether this remark was intended as criticism or as propaganda we need not stop to consider. What is important here is that Douglas's *Aeneid*, though it could not be other than unsatisfactory as a translation of Virgil's, *might* be a better poem than Virgil's.

Once the two *Aeneids* have been recognized as distinct, it might be supposed that a comparison between them would help towards a more critical enjoyment of each. But between poems of different languages there is seldom sufficient common ground on which to establish such a comparison. Thus it is not to Virgil's *Aeneid* but to the body of medieval Scots poetry that Douglas's *Aeneid* is immediately and organically related. Although the one is a fairly close translation of the other, Virgil's *Aeneid* and Douglas's are about as different as any other two poems in different European languages. What we should be attempting in comparing them would be something about as wide as a comparison between the Scots and the Latin languages; the difference between the two poems

69

being ultimately that between the Scots and Latin sensibilities. But we can begin to form a distinct particularization of Douglas's poem out from medieval Scots poetry in general only by comparing it with other medieval Scots poems. It may then become apparent how far the poem is affected by being a translation of a Latin poem, and how far as a consequence it extends the boundaries of Scots poetry, as Chaucer had done those of English poetry, in the direction—to use a geographical symbol of the Mediterranean.

Douglas's problem in the task he consciously set himself was primarily a problem of the selection and arrangement of words, but in that task was implied nothing less than an attempt to translate—to assimilate in Scots—a civilization. In the Prologue to Book I he shows that he was himself aware of the nature of his difficulties. By comparison with Virgil's metropolitan and polite Latin he perceives that Scots is rural ('rural vulgar gross') and barbarous ('lewit barbour tongue'). Here is a passage from Book V:

> Be than the auld Meneit[1] our schipburd slyde,
> Hevy, and all his weid sowpit with seis,
> Scars from the wattir ground upboltit he is,
> Syne swymmand held onto the craggis hycht,
> Sat on a dry rolk,[2] and hym self gan dycht.
> The Troianis lauchis fast seand hym fall,
> And, hym behaldand swym, thai keklit all;
> Bot maist thai maiking gem[3] and gret riot,
> To see hym spout salt wattir of his throt.

This (with for example its suggestion of hens in 'keklit') has a vigour that Virgil might have envied, but it is not 'polite'. There comes out in it that savage folk humour that comes out also in other medieval Scots poetry. Even if the first Prologue were not so explicit as it is, it might be assumed from Douglas's undertaking that Virgil's Latin must have made him conscious of a centre of polite and humane civilization in the past that might serve as a type of what Scots should seek to become. It was an attitude which was to persist throughout Europe right up to the beginning of the nineteenth century. Latin,

---

[1] Menoetes.   [2] rock.   [3] game.

which was to Dunbar the Latin of the medieval Catholic Church, was to Douglas the Latin *also* of the Roman Empire and its older civilization.[1]

Virgil was, of course, a sacred poet to the Middle Ages; there are signs that, at the beginning of the sixteenth century, he was ceasing to be so. But Douglas's oneness with the medieval poets may be felt in almost any of his lines. The description in Book IV of Dido and Aeneas passing to hunting offers a convenient comparison with Chaucer's version of the same in the *Legend of Good Women*. The resemblances between Douglas's poem and those of Chaucer and others are not merely a matter of unconscious reminiscence or conscious borrowing. The tenderness ('pitee') of the passage about the death of Euryalus and Nisus and the lament of the mother of Euryalus in Book IX correspond, of course, to the Virgilian tenderness, but are not quite the same; they are in the vein of the medieval Christian tenderness common in different degrees to Chaucer and Douglas and to all medieval poetry.

It would clear up many misconceptions if it could be established in what sense the original Prologues to the various books of Douglas's *Aeneid* are 'original' as compared with the 'translation' part of the poem.[2] In some respects the 'translation' part might be regarded as more 'original' than at least some passages of the Prologues. Douglas's indebtedness—which is immediately to his Scots predecessors—is even more apparent in these passages than in the translation. There is in some of these passages a more Latinized diction than there is anywhere in the translation from Virgil's Latin, and this Latinized diction (together with a French element) is the 'aureate diction' which had been formed in Scots, as in English, fifteenth-century poetry.

Yet Scots poetry, even medieval Scots poetry, has never been less provincial than the 'translation' part of Douglas's

[1] I now (1961) think I was mistaken in suggesting that Douglas had this kind of historical sense.

[2] Douglas's descriptions of the seasons certainly owe much to the *Georgics*.

Aeneid. The limitations within which Douglas worked, and which were recognized by him as limitations, were imposed not by Virgil but by the Scots language. But Middle Scots, as Douglas inherited it, and thanks to the work of his predecessors, could be compelled, recalcitrant though Douglas still felt it, to perform a task of what might be described as European significance and magnitude. Its very recalcitrance, its resistance through its power of individuality, became then in some respects a positive advantage. Douglas's Scots poem could *afford* to be more free from provinciality than even its immediate predecessors without losing its Scots identity. If it is even more free than they from provinciality we may conjecture that to be the effect the Latin poem had on it. But the difference between it and later Scots poems arises primarily from the fact that when this poem was written, Scotland was a growing branch of the growing tree that was Europe, and its language had temporarily taken its place as one of the literary languages of Europe.

No doubt Douglas brought across a modifying something from his direct experience of reading Virgil, though what that something was it would be difficult to analyse, since it was changed into something different again in the act of becoming Scots poetry. The 'originality' of the remarkable description of winter which forms the Prologue to Book VII is more easily estimable in relation to the work of Douglas's predecessors. It evidently *originates* in Douglas's own direct experience of the winter in Scotland. Henryson had previously made this region of winter a very actual presence in his poetry. We need only turn to the introductory passage of Henryson's *Fable of the Swallow and the Other Birds* to find a feeling for birds, beasts and humans overtaken by the winter, similar to that of the following passage from the Douglas Prologue:

> Smal byrdis, flokand throw thik ronnis[1] thrang,
> In chyrmyng and with cheping changit thair sang,
> Sekand hidlis[2] and hirnys[3] thaim to hyde
> Fra feirful thudis of the tempestuus tyde.

[1] briars, brambles.   [2] hiding places.   [3] corners.

> The wattir lynnis[1] routtis, and every lynde[2]
> Quhyslyt and brayt of the swouchand wynde.
> Puire laboraris and byssy husband men
> Went wayt and wery draglyt in the fen;
> The silly scheip and thair lytill hyrd gromis
> Lurkis vndir le of bankis, wodys, and bromys.

And we need only turn to the opening of the *Testament of Cresseid* for an apprehension of the cold season actual in much the same terms as those ('congealit', 'penetrative', 'pure', 'dazing the blood') of the following:

> In this congelyt sessioune scharp and chyll,
> The callour air, penetrative and puire,
> Dasyng the bluide in every creature,
> Maid seik warm stovis, and beyne fyris hoyt,
> In double garmont cled and wyly[3] coyt[3];
> Wyth mychty drink, and meytis confortive. . . .

But Douglas's descriptions are on a still larger scale, more cumulative, more massive:

> Reveris ran reid on spait with watteir broune,
> And burnis hurlis all thair bankis downe, . . .
> On raggit rolkis of hard harsk[4] quhyne stane,
> With frosyne frontis cauld clynty[5] clewis[6] schane; . . .
> Goustly schaddois of eild and grisly deid,
> Thik drumly scuggis dirknit so the hevyne. . . .
> Scharp soppis of sleit, and of the snypand snawe.
> The dowy dichis war all donk and wait,
> The law vaille flodderit all wyth spait,
> The plane stretis and every hie way
> Full of fluschis, dubbis, myre and clay.
> Laggerit[7] leys wallowit[8] farnys[9] schewe,
> Broune muris kithit[10] thair wysnit mossy hewe,
> Bank, bra, and boddum blanschit wolx and bair;
> For gurll weddir growyt bestis haire;
> The wynd maid wayfe the reid weyd on the dyk,
> Bedovin[11] in donkis deyp was every syk;[12]

[1] waterfalls.　　　　　[2] tree.
[3] short jacket, worn under vest in winter.　　　[4] rough.
[5] hard.　　[6] claws.　　[7] muddy, miry.　　[8] withered.
[9] ferns.　　[10] showed.　　[11] ? muddied.　　[12] stream.

73

Our craggis, and the front of rochis seyre,
Hang gret isch schoklis lang as ony spere;
The grund stude barrand, widderit, dosk and gray.

Though, in its medieval context, it gains much of its force[1] from
being 'ane similitude of hell' haunted by 'ghostly shadowis
of eild and grisly deid', the landscape, its burns in spate, its
'broun muiris' with 'wisnit mossy hue'—'The wind made
wave the reid weed on the dyke'—is unmistakably Scottish.
It was a difficult achievement for a medieval poet—if he was a
Scotsman or Englishman conscious of the poetry of Italy
and Provence, where medieval poetry had its roots—to be
so *local*. But in describing winter Douglas was forced back
more on his own resources, which happened to be what for
this purpose were the incomparable resources of his Scots
speech, than he was in his description of summer (Prologues
to Books XII and XIII). He experiences summer in his poetry
primarily as the Mediterranean summer—he writes of the olive
and the grape—which had penetrated into Scots, as into
English, poetry from the poetry of Provence and Italy. It is
the quality of the diction that distinguishes Douglas's poetic
summer from his winter. The 'aureate diction' of much of the
summer places it at once as the fashionable rhetoric of the late
fifteenth and early sixteenth centuries. The difference comes
out again in the nature of the alliteration and assonance,
which is more consciously manipulated in the case of the summer and less indigenous and organic. The 'gemmyt treis' and
the 'sylver scalyt' fishes in the 'cleir stremis' belong to the
allegorical landscapes. The fishes

Wyth fynnis schynand broun as synopar
And chyssell talis, stourand heyr and thar,

go back, in Scots, to the *Kingis Quair*, though they have lost
their original symbolic significance. But even Douglas's summer has its occasional particular observation:

Upgois the bak wyth hir pelit ledderyn flycht.

[1] The heavy, clogged rhythm suggests a huge, impeded, dammed-up
force.

It may not have been an accident that the poet of the *Seasons* was like the poet of these Prologues, a Scotsman, but though a Scotsman Thomson was not a Scots poet. That in itself sets Thomson and Douglas so far apart as to make the comparison between them, sometimes recommended, of little help. Unlike Thomson's Miltonic English, the un-Scottish elements in the literary language Douglas inherited could not prevent him from being a Scots poet even in his summer.

It is lucky that the British Muse can claim Douglas's *Aeneid*. Surrey's blank verse fragment has greater historical importance than poetic value. Dryden's heroic couplet *Aeneid* is in the inflated heroic style, and seems to me much inferior as a poem to Douglas's. But any English *Aeneid*, even in heroic couplets (even Pope's *Iliad*), was almost bound after Milton's epic to be in some degree Miltonic, and no Scots *Aeneid* comparable to Douglas's would have been possible later than the sixteenth century. In the treatment of a Classical theme in Scots, Henryson had already shown the capabilities of the language, as it then was, in parts of his *Orpheus and Eurydice*. His descent of Orpheus in that poem offers a comparison with Douglas's descent of Aeneas in Book VI. Although the later descent is fairly literal translation, it has again the essentially Scots and medieval quality of the Orpheus descent. There is the presence of the mythological folk-imagination of the Middle Ages as distinct from that of the Classical World:

> And in the middis of the utir ward,
> With braid branschis spred our all the sward,
> A rank elm tre stude, huge grit, and stok ald:
> The vulgair pepill in that sammyn hald[1]
> Belevis thir vane dremis makis thair duelling;
> Undir ilk leif full thik thai stik and hing.

The difference between that *vain* and *vana* is the difference between the two worlds. To appreciate that difference one must think of the word *vain* (Pride and Vanity) as used in the folk *Ballads*. Dryden, as belonging to the Age of Correctness,

[1] hold, place of shelter.

has the emptier 'empty'. The 'thick . . . stick . . . hing' of the richly physiological folk speech renders what is in the sophisticated Latin the concise precision of *haerent*, The shadows and the savage beasts

>Amang the schaddowis and the skuggis merk
>The hell houndis hard thai youll and berk.

and the monstrous shapes of Dreid, Age, Hunger, Indigence and Discord, among which Aeneas adventures, belong in Douglas's poem to the medieval Hell. (Virgil had been Dante's guide to his Hell.) Aeneas would have rushed upon those shapes with drawn sword,

>And with his bitand brycht brand, all in vane,
>The tume[1] schaddowis smytyn to have slane.

There is that surety and mastery in handling the great theme that Henryson had already shown. But never before or since has there been any other such sustained flight in Scots as these twelve books. They indicate in what was in some ways (if we are to judge from some of the evidence) the semi-barbarous Scotland of the early sixteenth century, the existence not only of a high level of humanistic scholarship but of a high level of culture, Scottish and European.

[1] empty.

6

David Lindsay

To explain David Lindsay's enormous popularity among
the Scottish people for almost two centuries after his
death—a popularity only equalled it is said by that of
the Bible—it would be necessary to enter into extra-literary
considerations. His verse (much of it seems to me dull) does
not in itself justify such popularity. Even at its best it is
inferior to Henryson and Dunbar and Gavin Douglas. The
more ambitious poems are in the dead conventional modes of
the early sixteenth century, and only locally does life assert
itself in them. It seems unlikely that it was on the strength of
these that Lindsay's popularity persisted after Henryson and
Dunbar were forgotten.

Lindsay's poems were so popular less, it seems, because of
their intrinsic merits than because politically they were on the
winning popular side (and *because* of their moralizings and
preachings, which included lengthy advice as to how the King
should govern). In Lindsay's hands the traditional satire
against Churchmen turned, whether intentionally or not, political as much as moral. It took effect at the most vulnerable
point—the growing corruption of the Church—as propaganda
of the social revolution which to a great extent the Reformation in Scotland was. The nature of Lindsay's satire as compared with Dunbar's (Lindsay's is more related to the possibility of political action) itself suggests the extent to which the
Reformation in Scotland was taking on the aspect of an up-
rising of the common people against ecclesiastical, legal and
other forms of a corrupt authority.

Heir sall they cleith Johne the Common-weil gorgeouslie and set him doun amang them in the Parliament.

In addition to the ecclesiastical satire turned political, the elements of Lindsay's work which probably appealed to the Scottish folk, were the moralizings and preachings, and the quite distinct comic, largely farcical, 'popular' element, broad and ribald. There is far more of this last, and, because in association with the 'right' moral and political attitudes of the more serious parts, it probably accounted for much more of the popularity than is conventionally assumed. Of these elements there is of course no poetic value in the prosy prolix moralizings which were evidently found edifying in the post-Reformation period. There remain the satiric and comic passages. The chief task of criticism will be to separate these out from the dead mass of Lindsay's work.

Of the longer non-dramatic poems the one which is quite free from dead conventional matter and which, although far too long, can still be read with fresh enjoyment is the *Complaynt*. The passages about the childhood of James V would commend themselves even to those who are not interested in 'poetry'.

> Quhow, as ane Chapman beris his pak,
> I bure thy grace upon my bak,
> And, sumtymes, strydlingis[1] on my nek,
> Dansand with mony bend and bek.
> The first sillabis that thow did mute
> Was *pa, Da Lyn*: upon the lute
> Than playt I twenty spryngis, perqueir.[2]

But Lindsay does not indulge for long in tender personal memories and the recurring note is a certain harshness of virile common sense.

> Imprudentlie, lyk wytles fullis,
> Thay tuke that young Prince frome the sculis,
> Quhare he, under Obedience,
> Was lernand vertew and science,
> And haistelie plat[3] in his hand
> The governance of all Scotland.

[1] astride.   [2] by heart.   [3] put.

The *Complaynt* is a poem in the familiar conversational manner, but with the metrical and rhyming liveliness appropriate to the vernacular speech to which it owes its freedom and life.

> Sum gart him raiffel[1] at the rakat;[2]
> Sum harld hym to the hurly hakat;[3]
> And sum, to schaw thare courtlie corsis,
> Wald ryid to Leith, and ryn thare horssis,
> And wychtlie wallope[4] ouer the sandis.

The poem shows most of Lindsay's positive qualities at once, for his total successful work when separated out from the rest of his work is much more limited in range than at first sight appears. Though within Lindsay's more limited achievement itself there is sufficient variety, as I hope to show, to indicate that it is a living organism, there is nothing of the variety of achievement of Dunbar, just as there is not the same intensity of power at any one point. The satire in the *Complaynt*, for instance, suggests a comparison with Dunbar's because its phrases are reminiscent of Dunbar's, but on the whole, if in a sense more narrowly 'interested', Lindsay's satire is weaker, as what tends to be reminiscent generally is. Still, if not equal to Dunbar, the *Complaynt* exhibits Lindsay's lively satiric gift and acrid comic sense.

The same could be said of *Syde Taillis* and *Kittie's Confession* among the shorter poems and for the same reason,

> To rurall folke myne dyting bene directed.

In so far as Lindsay adopts the speech of the peasantry, as he does generously in these poems, he ceases to be 'literary' and pretentious and ceases at once to be dull. *In Contemtion of Syde Taillis*—'a rurall ryme'—is less in the service of the will than any other single poem of Lindsay. Though professedly a satire on an unpractical fashion of women's dress—

> Of ane small falt, quilk is nocht Tressoun,
> Thocht it be contrarie to Ressoun.

---

[1] raffle, lounge about. [2] racket.
[3] sledging or sliding down steep place. [4] gallop.

—it is less really that than a giving rein to the coarse comic
zest inseparable from the peasant speech.

> Pure Claggokis[1] cled in roiploch[2] quhyte,
> Quhilk hes skant twa markis for thair feis,
> Will have twa ellis beneth thare kneis.
> Kittok, that clekkit[3] wes yestreen,
> The morne, wyll counterfute the Quene.
> Ane mureland Meg, that milkis the yowis,
> Claggit[4] with clay abone the howis,[5]
> In barn nor byir scho will nocht byde,
> Without her kirtyll taill be syde.
> In Burrowis, wantoun burges wyiffis,
> Quha may have sydest taillis stryiffis,
> Weill bordourit with velvoit fyne . . .
> Than, quhen thay step furth throw the streit,
> Thair faldingis[6] flappis about thair feit,
> Thair laithlie lyning furthwart flypit,[7]
> Quhilk hes the muk and midding wypit.

Of the coarseness Lindsay has felt it necessary to be explanatory:

> Because the Matter bene so vyle,
> It may nocht have ane Ornate style . . .
> Of stinkand weidis maculate,[8]
> Na man may mak ane Rois Chaiplate.

The freedom from the ornate style is in itself a positive gain.
As for the presence of what the modern reader may find
offensive, there is enough vigorous positive enjoyment to be
got from the elements co-present with this offensive element
to outweigh it. *Kittie's Confession*, though equally 'popular', is
more evidently traditional than *Syde Taillis*, and the best part
of it might perhaps be by anyone. The opening dialogue between the Curate and Kittie ('The Curate Kittie wald have
kist') gives its goliardic character to the poem,

> And mekle Latyne he did mummill
> I hard na thing but hummill bummill,

but the indictment of the Church turns earnest.

[1] ? clogged, muddled individuals.   [2] coarse, undyed woollen cloth.
[3] hatched (i.e. born).   [4] clogged, muddied.
[5] houghs, backs of thighs.   [6] garments of coarse woollen cloth.
[7] turned inside out.   [8] foul.

Ane Satyre of the Thrie Estaitis invites special attention as the only considerable dramatic piece preserved in Scots. Scots poetry has perhaps a more dramatic character than English poetry as a whole has had, at any rate since the seventeenth century; it is more related to speech and action on the one hand as also to song and dance on the other. But if we look to Lindsay's play as evidence of the great dramatic poetry there might have developed in Scots parallel with the English we shall be disappointed. It will be observed that it is no interesting new local departure. It is simply a by no means promising modification, in some respects dissipation, of the Morality tradition. *Ane pleasant Satyre of the Thrie Estaitis in commendatioun of Vertew and Vituperatioun of Vyce* shows considerable uncertainty of purpose resulting in considerable disorganization, but in so far as it is a 'Morality' it is again deflected to political as much as moral ends. My own experience is that it is difficult to read *through*.[1] But again, as is the case with Lindsay's poetry as a whole, in the midst of so much that is dead, there are sudden passages of abundant life. These passages are almost invariably the passages of 'popular' comedy or, more strictly, farce. Occasionally they are coarse to the point of a brutality not found even in Dunbar. As the considerable variety in the verse of these passages reflects, there is in them within the 'popular' limits, a considerable variety of kinds of comedy and satire most of them traditional in origin.

The recognition of this limited variety of local successes is what, after high claims for it as a whole play or even for most of its parts have been abandoned, may engage criticism. Already the prelude to the play provides goodish popular farce of the *chanson à mal mariée* tradition in the dialogue between the Cotter and his Wife, who have both gone to Cowper to see the play.

> Quhair hes thou bene, fals ladrone loun?
> Doyttand and drinkand in the toun,
> Quha gaif the leif to cum fra hame?

[1] It is fair to say that since I wrote this the play has been performed, and surprised those who witnessed it with its power to hold the attention (1961).

She continues in the manner of the *Wife of Auchtermuchty*:

> Swyth cairle, speid the hame speidaly,
> Incontinent, and milk the ky,
> And muk the byre or I cum hame.

There is a less simple example—involving this same type of traditional farce—in the play itself at a point where the purely human figures are brought into farcical collision with a personification belonging to the 'Morality' element. The Sowtar and the Taylor sit down to drink with Chastitie.

> SOWTAR. Fill in and play cap' out,[1]
> For I am wonder dry;
> The Devill snyp aff thair snout,
> That haits this company.
> [*Heir sall thay gar chestety sit doun and drink.*]

Jennie, the Taylor's daughter, catches sight of them and calls out to her mother:

> Hoaw, mynnie, mynnie, mynnie.[2]
> TAYLOR'S WIFE. Quhat wald thou my deir dochter Jennie?
> Jennie my Joy, quhair is thy dadie?
> JENNIE. Mary drinkand with ane lustie ladie
> Ane fair young mayden cled in quhyte.

The Sowtar's wife[3] next enters, and together the wives put Chastitie to flight—

> CHASTITIE. Marie, Chastitie is my name be Sanct Blais.
> TAYLOR'S WIFE. I pray God nor he work on the vengence
> For I luifit never Chastitie all my dayes—

and 'ding their gudemen' who conclude the episode with the traditional complaint of the evils of being 'weddit with sic wicket wyvis'. Farce of a similar kind is provided elsewhere by a *Miles gloriosus*[4] who after his boastings and rant is routed by a sheepshead.

> I trow yone be grit gowmakmorne,
> He gaippis, he glowris; howt welloway.

---

[1] empty the cup.   [2] mother.
[3] Cf. Noah's wife and Mak's wife in the Miracle Plays.
[4] Cf. Herod and his like in the Miracle Plays.

A dialogue between Pauper and Diligence provides an example of the traditional 'flyting', while at the same time illustrating, in the extraordinary clowning of Pauper, popular impudence asserting itself against age-old authority.

PAUPER. Quha Devil maid the ane gentill man that wald not cut thy lugs?
DILIGENCE. Quhat now? Me thinks the carle begins to crack,
Swyith[1] carle, away, or be this day Ise break thy back.
[*Heir sall the Carle clim up and sit on the Kings tchyre.*]
Cum doun, or be Gods croun, fals loun, I sall slay the.
PAUPER. Now sweir be thy brunt[2] schinis, the Devill ding them fra the.
Quhat say ye till thir court dastards? Be thay get hail clais,
Sa sune do thay leir to sweir and trip on thair tais.
DILIGENCE. Me thocht the carle callit me knave evin in my face.
Be Sanct Fillane thou salbe slane, bot gif thou ask grace;
Loup doun or be the gude Lord thow sall los thy heid.
PAUPER. I sal anis drink or I ga thocht thou had sworne my deid.
[*Heir Diligence castes away the ledder.*]
DILIGENCE. Loup now gif thou list, for thou hes lost the ledder.
PAUPER. It is full weil thy kind to loup and licht in a ledder;[3]
Thow sal be faine to fetch agane the ledder or I loup.
I sall sit heir into this tchyre till I have tumde[4] the stoup.
[*Heir sall the Carle loup aff the scaffald.*]

There are a number of mock 'Confessions' of which the jolliest is, as might be expected, a Pardoner's

I am Sir Robert Rome-raker,
Ane perfite publike pardoner,
Admittit be the Paip.

His speech performing his deceptions for the entertainment of the audience, who are not deceived, belongs with the 'confessions' of medieval comic and satiric poetry. Though conventionalized, his 'confession' is at the same time sufficiently localized, with a distinct earthy character.

Of Collings cow heir is ane horne;
For eating of Makconnals corne,

[1] quickly.   [2] burnt, i.e. wounded, blistered.
[3] an indecent pun.   [4] emptied.

Was slaine into Baquhidder.
Heir is ane coird baith great and lang,
Quhilk hangit Johne the Armistrang,
Of gude hemp soft and sound;
Gude halie peopill I stand for'd,
Quha ever beis hangit with this cord,
Neids never to be dround.
The culum of Sanct Brydis kow,
The gruntile[1] of Sanct Antonis sow,
Quhilk buir his haly bell;
Quha ever he be heiris this bell clinck
Gif me ane ducat for till drink,
He sall never gang to hell.

There is a considerable element from the popular Bird and
Beast Fables in the play even if it does not adopt the most
obvious forms. The wolf-in-sheepskin conception persists, and
considerable use is made of disguises. Such traditional 'morality' figures as Flatterie, Falset, Deceit, disguise themselves in
the hoods of monks and friars.[2] This fits in with the additional
purpose of enforcing the satire against Churchmen. The most
actual satire in the play is that which arises from a sense of the
sufferings and grievances of the poor, and it is concentrated
chiefly in John the Commonweal's 'Complaints' of the wrongs
and injustices suffered by the common people at the hands of
the Church and the Law. When enumerating (among those who
do no 'honest' work)

Fidlers, pypers, and pardoners:
Thir jugglars, jestars, and idill cuitchours,[3]
Thir carriers[4] and thir quintacensours:[5]
Thir babil-beirers[6] and thir bairds,[7]
Thir sweir swyngeours[8] with Lords and Lairds.

Lindsay reminds one of Dunbar's flytings (though he has not
Dunbar's language at large), but when he passes to attack
monks and friars—

[1] snout.

[2] Cf. in the *Testament of the Papyngo* the birds as monks, friars, priests,
canons.

[3] sluggards.   [4] jugglers.   [5] seekers after the quintessence.
[6] fools.   [7] bards.   [8] swingers, scoundrels.

This bene against the great fat Freiris
Augustenes, Carmleits and Cordeleirs
And all uthers that in cowls bene cled,
Quhilk labours nocht and bene weill fed . . .
Lyand in dennis lyke idill doggis
I them compair to weil fed hoggis

—the vituperation becomes angry in a more individual way. This angry note is taken up again, though with more humour, in Pauper's 'complaint' against the Law's obstructions.

They gave me first ane thing thay call citandum,
Within aucht dayis I gat bot lybellandum,
Within ane moneth I gat ad opponendum,
In half ane yeir I gat interloquendum,
And syne I gat, how call ye it? ad replicandum,
Bot I could never ane word yit understand him.

The lawless figures of Common Theft and Oppression possess a certain half-farcical violent life (it exists of course in their language) which together with the half-farcical violence of the hangings seem to be representative of aspects of the actual state of Scotland that had acquired a hold on the 'popular' imagination. Falsit's 'testament' when he is about to be hanged is one of the liveliest—as when he speaks of a kind of ale made by the 'brousters of Cowper toun'.

Ane curtill[1] queine,[2] ane laidlie[3] lurdane,[4]
Of strang wesche[5] scho will tak ane jurdane
    And settis in the gyle-fat.[6]
Quha drinks of that aill, man or page,
It will gar all his harnis[7] rage.
    That jurdane I may rew;
It gart my heid rin hiddie giddie,
Sirs God nor I die in ane widdie,[8]
    Gif this taill be nocht trew.
Speir at the Sowtar Geordie Sillie,
Fra tyme that he had fild his bellie,
    With this unhelthsum aill.

[1] short-skirted, i.e. sluttish wanton.   [2] quean, jade.
[3] loathly.   [4] sot, lazy lout.   [5] urine.
[6] vat in which the wort is left to ferment.   [7] brains.
[8] withy, gallows-rope.

The play ends—the figures of the Fool and the King having been brought together—in a kind of rough festival of fools. The last words with their announcement that now that the play is ended everyone is at length free 'to rin to the tavern incontinent' are a curious *finale* to a Morality. In all this (and I have of course left out of account the moralizings and preachings that form the bulk of the play) it is useless to attempt to see much unity other than as varieties of popular comedy and satire. There are resemblances to the kind of play that at one time I thought Mr. Auden might write. The difference is that a modern is cut off from these traditional roots (which I have been attempting to indicate) and I doubt if they could be consciously come by. In so far as Lindsay's popularity was not extra-literary, in so far as the Scottish people were enjoying literature in reading his work, those passages related to the tradition of popular vernacular poetry that persists and grows into Burns are what justify it. This reduces Lindsay's claims greatly by comparison with Dunbar and Henryson (in Lindsay the 'literary' Scots poetry is quite dead) but leaves him, if ever he is submitted to a critical examination, a secure position as a genuine 'popular' poet of a limited order.

7

Sixteenth-century Scots Poems

ALEXANDER SCOTT

That the 'literary' Scots poetry of the sixteenth century, in general moribund in the medieval modes, could still in one or two instances possess itself of renewed vitality is shown by the songs and lyrics of Alexander Scott. They correspond to Wyatt's in the English tradition. They are in some ways less Petrarchan conventional, and more bodied, less purely lover's laments, than the general run of sixteenth-century songs and sonnets. They indicate that the 'literary' Scots tradition still had it in it to continue parallel with the English and the European tradition. That it did not, but that in Drummond it converged not simply into identity with but into an external imitation of the English tradition, cannot be explained from itself.

The vigorous individual character of Alexander Scott's songs is not more remarkable than their accomplished skill. They are 'literary' songs, selections of words arranged according to intricate metrical patterns and with refrains which have not a purely metrical value but (as in the distinct Scottishness of 'I find ye aye so nice') concentrate the meaning. This Scots art goes back ultimately to the *canzon de l'amour courtois* of the troubadours; the poet may be supposed to have a musical pattern in his mind which the words follow. But the words have their full value as words.

The movement is even more that of dance, but has not the abandon of folk-dance; part of the energy is used up in the intricacy of the art which thereby contributes to the maintenance of an air of aristocratic self-possession. Literary poetry in the sixteenth century was essentially the product of one social class—the aristocratic—and shared the tone of that class. But in the sixteenth century the aristocracy was still not merely in proximity to, but in actual connection with, the peasant people, and Alexander Scott's songs which are 'literary' poetry—poetry essentially of a cultivated aristocratic circle—share, while remaining aloof and self-possessed, a certain element of the 'popular'.

> Whatten ane glaikit fule am I
> To slay myself with melancholy,
>   Sen weill I ken I may nocht get her!
> Or what suld be the cause, and why,
>   To brek my hairt, and nocht the better.

This sobering self-knowledge—in contrast to the Petrarchan hyperbolical extravagance—does it arise from the shrewdness of the popular speech and mind or from hard sixteenth-century aristocratic sophistication? Sometimes it appears more the one, sometimes more the other, but in these songs the two are never wholly distinguishable.

It is not ingenuity of thought which is present so much as a steadying ballast of experienced, often sceptical, wisdom. While testifying to the strength of passion equally to a Burns song, Alexander Scott, in his songs, takes a more detached view. The violence of passion is pitted against an absence of illusionment which indicates the persisting effectiveness of medieval religious and moral tradition. There are sharp contrasts of feeling and attitude in Scott's songs, and often a certain harshness of judgment.

ALEXANDER BOYD

Alexander Boyd's *Sonnet*, though it belongs to almost a generation later, represents still an alliance between scholarly accomplishment and vigorous 'popular' qualities.

Fra bank to bank, fra wood to wood I rin,
Ourhailit with my feeble fantasie;
Like til a leaf that fallis from a tree,
Or til a reed ourblawin with the win.
Twa gods guidis me: the ane of tham is blin,
Yea and a bairn brocht up in vanitie;
The neist a wife ingenrit of the sea,
And lichter nor a dauphin with her fin.
Unhappy is the man for evermair
That tills the sand and sawis in the air;
But twice unhappier is he, I lairn,
That feidis in his hairt a mad desire,
And followis on a woman throw the fire,
Led by a blin and teachit by a bairn.

The traditional religious wisdom—not simply Puritanism but something much older—has here gained the dominance and is responsible for a deeper, a religious, seriousness registered in such words as 'fantasie' and 'vanitie' and in the phrases 'lichter nor a dauphin with her fin', 'tills the sand', 'sawis the air', 'fedis in his hairt a mad desire', 'followis on a woman throw the fire', modified by the Scots idiom that turns Cupid to a 'bairn' and Venus to a 'wife'. There is a harshness in this religious contempt for human frailty that contrasts with the medieval Christian courtly tenderness of feeling—gentleness as well as courtliness—of Dunbar's *To a Ladie*. These poets continue the tradition—the central European tradition in Scots—by each modifying it.

ALEXANDER HUME[1]

It becomes even more evident that Scottish poetry just before it was abandoned by the aristocracy and the cultivated was capable of new beginnings when we examine Alexander Hume's poem *Of the Day Estivall*. A new mode of apprehension

[1] I have left this section on Hume's poem unchanged (exactly as it was when published in 1940) and invite the reader to compare it with pages 124–5 of Dr. Kurt Wittig's *The Scottish Tradition in Literature* (1958).

is behind its apparent simplicity. The purity of the poet's sensibility is shown in the exactness and clarity with which forms and colours are reflected as in a mirror or still pool. To the sixteenth-century humanist objects have become detachable for curious, already almost 'scientific' observation. The objects—their properties and mechanisms—are recorded with a new kind of precision.

> Back from the blue paymented whun,
>   And from ilk plaister wall,
> The hot reflexing of the sun
>   Inflames the air and all . . .
> With gilded eyes and open wings,
>   The cock his courage shaws,
> With claps of joy his breast he dings
>   And twenty times he craws.
> The dow with whistling wings sa blue
>   The winds can fast collect,
> His purpour pennes turns mony hue
>   Against the sun direct.

This originality of apprehension registers itself in the vocabulary. In their context the latinisms are not those of the 'aureate diction'; they are not ornamental but technical. The landscape as a whole has, as proceeding from the nature of the observation, a curiously static quality.[1]

> The ample heaven of fabric sure
>   In cleanness does surpass
> The crystall and the silver pure
>   Or clearest poleist glass . . .
> All trees and simples great and small
>   That balmy leaf do bear,
> Nor they were painted on a wall
>   Na mair they move or steir.
> Calm is the deep and purpour sea,
>   Yea, smoother nor the sand;
> The wawis that welt'ring wont to be,
>   Are stable like the land.
> Sa silent is the cessile air,
>   That every cry and call,

[1] Cf. in the previous passage the almost metallic quality of the Cock ('gilded eyes', 'dings').

> The hills, and dales, and forest fair
>> Again repeats them all . . .
> The stable ships upon the sea
>> Tends up their sails to dry . . .
> The reek thraws right up in the air
>> From every tower and town . . .
> What pleasure were to walk and see,
>> Endlang a river clear,
> The perfite form of every tree
>> Within the deep appear.

Perhaps, because of their emphasis on 'stability' (compare 'the stable ships upon the sea'), the most significant lines in the poem are:

> The wawis that welt'ring wont to be,
> Are stable like the land.

if we remember that poem after poem previously has registered the sense of Mutability and perpetual flux. It is a secular landscape deliberately, unhurriedly particularized; but the feeling which is kept distinct and to which the objective precision of the observation is subordinated is that of a consecrated and holy enjoyment, a quiet profound piety. Integrity of this kind—suggested in another aspect by Alexander Hume's Platonic attitude to poets—

> Ye pride your pens men's ears to please
> With fables and fictitious lees

—seems to be both rationalist and Puritan. Observation of the Universe controlled by the Reason and directed as pious adoration towards a First Cause, familiar as it was to become in the seventeenth and eighteenth centuries, was something new in Scots sixteenth-century poetry. The older religious poetry, by comparing Hume's poem with which we may see more clearly what was lost in the change, may fairly be represented by the lines

> O my deir hart, yung Jesus sweit
> Prepair thy creddill in my spreit,
> And I sall rock thee in my hart
> And never mair fra thee depart.

> Bot I sall praise thee evermoir
> With sangis sweit unto thy gloir
> The kneis of my hart sall I bow
> And sing that rycht Balulalow.

These lines, though appearing in 1567 in the Protestant *Gude and Godly Ballads*, are essentially of the medieval Catholic folk in their symbolism and tenderness.

SIR RICHARD MAITLAND

Sir Richard Maitland's verse, unless in that part of it (*Though I be Auld*,[1] for example) which comes nearest to the vernacular verse of the eighteenth century—thus already in the sixteenth beginning to separate out—shows rather a last mellow ripening of the past than a new promise.

His MS. collection (by which a number of the most valuable Middle Scots poems have been preserved) is sufficient to prove him to have been a man of taste. That, when blind and old, he took pains to have copies made of these poems suggests he may have felt that they were no longer valued as they had been, and that there was some danger of their loss. But the directest evidence of his having had a sense of the immediate pastness of a valuable past is that of certain of his own poems in which there is a sadness of regretfulness that reminds one they were written in the reign of Mary. Maitland's satires bear a relation to Dunbar's. But his *Satire on the Age*, for example, is without the acridness of Dunbar. The quality of this softening is apparent in the note of 'Quhair is the blythness that hes bein' on which the poem opens. Not that there can be any weakening sentimentally co-present with such strength and freedom of mind as proceeds from Maitland's character and

---

[1] Here is a stanza from *Though I be Auld*:

> The fairest wench in all this toun
> Though I her had in her best gown
> Richt bravely brall'd,
> With her I micht not play the loun,
> I am sa auld.

experience and perhaps also from his considerable affinity with the 'popular' mind. In his *Satire on the Town Ladies* this affinity comes out in his sense of the 'vanity' of costly silks and velvets; and in *Aganis the Theivis of Liddisdaill* in a certain glee in the rhythm which suggests a partial identification of the old judge (Maitland was a judge of the Court of Session) with the thieves. That Maitland is a genuine poet the following from *Na Kyndnes at Court without Siller*[1] may show:

> To ane grit court-man I did speir,
>   That I trowit my freind had bene
> Because we war of kyn sa neir;
>   To him my mater I did mene;
>   Bot with disdene,
>   He fled as I had done him tene,
> And wald nocht byd my taill to heir.

> My hand I put into my sleif,
>   And furthe of it ane purs I drew,
> And said I brocht it him to geif.
>   Bayth gold and siller I him schew;
>   Than he did rew
>   That he unkindlie me misknew;
> And hint the purs fest in his neif.

> Fra tyme he gat the purs in hand
>   He kyndlie 'Cosin' callit me,
> And baid me gar him understand
>   My buseness all haillalie,
>   And swair that he
>   My trew and faythfull freind sould be
> In courte as I pleis him command.

If it is considered that this was written a generation before Donne the distinction of the Scottish poem may be measured. The poise, the resultant of the balance held between the movement as that of speech and at the same time as intricately metrical, is perfect. The poem is both speech and verse—a

---

[1] It stands comparison with *Tydingis fra the Sessioun*, one of Dunbar's best satiric poems.

difficult achievement. This maturity of the art is but an aspect of the mature tone of the poem as a whole which arises from a wise maturity of mind.

ALEXANDER MONTGOMERIE

By comparison with the poetry of Scott, Boyd, Hume, and Maitland, that of Alexander Montgomerie exhibits considerable uncertainty and insecurity. Though constantly harking back to medieval modes (*O luvesome lady*, for example, is— though a profane poem—on the model of the hymns to the Virgin) it is beginning to be in places Renaissance poetry, and, though still in Scots, it leads on to the purely English imitation work of Drummond of Hawthornden. The unsatisfactoriness seems to arise—in spite of Montgomerie's technical preoccupation and artistry—from some inner weakening and impoverishment. The conscious artistic elaboration, as elaborate as a courtly and scholarly gentleman can work it, covers what is essentially simpler, less subtle, than the previous Scots poetry. The fact that it is possible to feel, as well as to think of, the artistry as separate from what else there is in the poem is not a good sign. The metrical skill itself becomes in places mere metricality; the metre seems to detach itself, as it were, from the poem and to lose relation with the mood. The jig movement which closes each stanza of the *Bankis of Helicon* and *The Cherry and the Slae* is as often as not shockingly inappropriate, as never in the Scots idiom of Burns, who with sure instinct adopted it. *The Cherry and the Slae*, on which Montgomerie's considerable reputation seems to be based, far too long in any case, bogs itself in moralizings but is at the same time fundamentally not serious enough. The prettiness, the charming littleness of his Cupid may be delicious but remains essentially trivial by comparison with the medieval lover's saint.

> Lo, how that little God of Love
> Before me there appeared!
> So mild-like and child-like,

With bow three quarteris scant,
So moyly and coyly,
   He lukit like ane sant.

Ane cleirly crisp hang owre his eyes,
His quiver by his naked thighs
   Hang in ane silver lace.
Of gold, betwix his shoulders, grew
Twa pretty wings wherewith he flew;
   On his left arm ane brace.

'What wald thou give me, friend,' quod he,
'To have thae pretty wingis to flee,
   To sport thee for a while?
Or what, gif I suld len' thee here
My bow and all my shooting gear,
   Somebody to beguile?'

    .   .   .   .

Than furth I drew that deadly dairt
Whilk sometime shot his mother,
Wherewith I hurt my wanton hairt,
   In hope to hurt ane other.

Montgomerie occasionally makes a pretty use of Renaissance Pagan Classical imagery, and his poetry is as a whole animated by a certain young delight. That is about the most that can be said. Montgomerie is at his best, it seems to me, in the song *Hey! Now the day dawis* where he is more nearly content to be freshly what he feels. But this song is simpler than most of Alexander Scott.

There were, then, a number of minor Scots poets of distinction in the sixteenth century who do not simply write in the manner of Dunbar, Henryson or Douglas. They show that the tradition of poetry-making in Scots could renew, not merely repeat, itself. There is nothing in this poetry itself to suggest that it was about to come to an almost complete stop. What is the explanation of the sudden falling away from the long-established practice of verse-making in Scots? It cannot have been an accident that the poets singled out in this chapter were aristocrats. The Court circle evidently provided at least

95

the nucleus of a cultivated audience for poetry in Scots. Not that the Scots poetry of the sixteenth century had become merely sophisticated. Its strength had been that it could be both sophisticated and popular. But it looks as though there could no longer be such an art of poetry in Scots in the seventeenth century when there was no longer a Scottish Court.

Christis Kirk on the Green and Peblis to the Play

The first notable poems in which the specific vernacular tradition that was to culminate in Fergusson and Burns may be observed in one of its particular forms are *Christis Kirk on the Green* and *Peblis to the Play*.

> Hopcalyo and Cardronow
> Gadderit out thick-fauld,
> With 'hey and how rolumbelow'
> The young folk were full bauld.
> The bagpipe blew, and they out-threw
> Out of the tounis untauld.

In the 'popular' verse there is no lack of joyous vitality at least, because no lack of it in the peasant people. Their fairs were their rustic Pagan festivals. About these there was nothing Puritan. The coarse, comic topsyturvydom of the fair is caught up into the wild abandon, the fling of the fast dance.

> He start to his great grey mare,
> And off he tumblit the creelis.
> 'Alas!' quod she, 'Hald our gudeman!'
> And on her knees she kneelis.
> 'Abide,' quod she; 'Why, nay,' quod he;
> In-till his stirrupis he lap;
> The girdin brak, and he flew off,
> And upstart baith his heelis,
>   At anis,
> Of Peblis to the play.

96

> His wife came out, and gaif ane shout,
> And be the fit she gat him;
> All bedirtin drew him out;
> 'Lord God! richt weil that sat him!'
> He said, 'Where is yon culroun knave?'
> Quod she, 'I rede ye, lat him
> Gang hame his gates.' 'Be God,' quod he,
> 'I sall anis have at him
> Yit,
> Of Peblis to the play.'

The rhythm and the continual series of surprising accidents heaped one on top of the other suggest an unstopping dance. The language, because it is that of peasant speech sharing the vigours of the abounding peasant life, magnificently conveys the sense of strongly physical, furious fun. The popular character of *Christis Kirk on the Green* and *Peblis to the Play* is of course no evidence that they were not composed by King James V to whom they were at one time attributed. The king would not be so dissociated from the folk that he would not have been capable of composing poetry not only in a 'popular' mode, but genuinely 'popular'.

8

The Scots Seventeenth Century

In the sixteenth century the medieval Catholic Scotland began to give way to (on the surface at least) Presbyterian Scotland. The profound nature of the changes (more radical than in England) which were then initiated, the dissolution of the whole organism and the severance of its vital connections with Europe, was bound to have the severest repercussions on poetry. It was not a coincidence that the cultivation of poetry in Scots as a serious 'literary' art among the aristocracy ceased in the seventeenth century. The most immediate cause was probably the transference of the Scottish court to England; for that deprived the Scottish aristocracy, and the art of poetry, of a Scottish centre. Gradually those of the aristocracy who continued to live only on their estates tended to become mere rustic landowners, while those who followed the court to England gradually lost, and were content to lose, their Scottish speech and individuality. What little distinctively Scots poetry persisted in the seventeenth century was already, even when cultivated by aristocrats, 'popular' in character.

Poetry as a serious 'literary' art began in the seventeenth century to be cultivated by Scottish aristocrats such as Drummond of Hawthornden, the friend of Ben Jonson, in English. Drummond wrote verse distinguishable from that of some of his English contemporaries only by being—as the inflexibility of the rhythm, the ornamental 'poetic' of the imagery reveal—an exceptionally accomplished and refined imitation of theirs. From Drummond's verse it is possible to see how Milton was destined to exert a fatal influence on

Scotsmen writing English verse. Drummond's successor in the more bourgeois eighteenth century was Thomson.

The English Bible also,[1] established early in the seventeenth century as the book most frequented by the Scottish people, destroyed the possibility of a Scots prose just when it had begun to develop with some vigour for vituperative controversial purposes. Hitherto the Latin of the Catholic Church, reinforced by the French influence (of the 'Auld Alliance'), had counteracted the English influence; but now, while the Catholic partisans wrote in Scots, the Protestants (being in alliance with Protestant England) began to write in English. The extinction of Scots prose, besides being deplorable in itself, was bound to affect unfavourably the development of Scots poetry. Actually the 'popular' poetry persisted for another two hundred years, dependent only on peasant speech (and song and dance). But a solid basis of prose would have been invaluable; for poetry could no longer continue, as before, satisfactorily to perform also the work of prose. So the anomaly arose of Scotsmen writing prose in English and verse in Scots. The absence of a Scots prose meant that certain faculties of the mind were denied their appropriate expression in Scots. Certain forms of thinking could not be done in Scots, because no Scots prose had been developed for such uses. There has never been, for example—though some of the Edinburgh reviewers of 1800 realized the need—a Scots criticism of Scots poetry; a Scots critical vocabulary had no chance to develop, nor a Scots philosophical or scientific vocabulary. The damage must have been incalculable; Scots poetry, since the medieval unity of it was broken up, lost touch with the currents of thought—partly owing to this absence of an intellectual vocabulary such as could only have been developed in a prose discipline.

[1] The English Bible had of course a profound influence on the lives and characters of Scottish folk and (as Wordsworth noted) on their speech:

> With something of a lofty utterance drest . . .
> Such as grave Livers do in Scotland use.

The explanation that it was because of the distraction of civil war that poetry was not cultivated in Scots in the seventeenth century is not in itself adequate. The history of Scotland before, and right up to, the sixteenth century is one of blood. In addition to the long feud with England, there were deep divisions within Scotland itself—the division between the Celtic Highlands and the Lowlands and the murderous feuds between the overpowerful barons involving incessantly the king; there was scarcely a Stuart king of Scotland who died in his bed. Yet in spite of that—because there was on the one hand a strong peasant life and on the other, in Catholicism, something European, and because there was a centre for it in the existence of a Scottish court—poetry was cultivated with greater success in the fifteenth century than in any later period.

It is more likely that the fanatical theological and political divisions and controversies of the seventeenth century ultimately restricted poetry in Scotland (though they were not what stultified the Scots prose) by in some way fragmenting the Scottish mind; they certainly produced an argumentative and partisan type of mind, a 'party-colour'd Mind'.[1] But there is no immediate evidence of this in the poetry itself. There is only the fact, which may simply be coincidental, that the cultivation of poetry in Scots as a 'literary' art rather abruptly ceased about the same time as these controversies. As far as the poetry which continued to be composed is concerned, whether that which was composed in English or the 'popular' poetry in Scots, there might almost have been no such thing as Calvinistic Presbyterianism. Puritanism is supposed to have been strongest among the people, yet the 'popular' poetry is in itself quite unaffected by it. The poetry belongs essentially to the older medieval half-Catholic, half-pagan Scottish community which evidently, to some extent, survived even the radical changes of the sixteenth and seventeenth centuries. Yet poetry in Scots since the seventeenth century remained confined to a few 'popular' modes perhaps because of the narrowing of interests, together with the limiting conception

[1] Marvell's *Horatian Ode.*

of poetry in Scots as 'rhyming' and 'fun', consequent upon the blow which in the seventeenth century was struck at the roots of humane culture. But the fact that poetry in Scotland had become split up into two kinds in different languages, itself indicates already a rupture, a cleavage in the essential unity of the nation, and of its mind and culture. The peasantry continued Scottish longest but was all but abandoned at the top.

PART TWO

Eighteenth-century Scots Verse

Allan Ramsay, Fergusson and Burns—in that chronological order—are the three outstanding makers of Scots verse in the eighteenth century. These poets are not remarkable as innovators. They work within the narrowly defined limits of a comparatively few modes, conventions and attitudes which they have inherited from the past of Scots verse. Their resemblances to each other are partly to be explained by the fact that they share the same modes, conventions and attitudes, and do not move outside them. It was perhaps in some ways to the advantage of their poetry that it was thus somewhat sharply defined and shaped. The spontaneous life and character of their poetry, for which it is indeed remarkable, are those of their spoken Scots out of which, within these definite limits, their poetry was made.

Ramsay, Fergusson and Burns were perhaps less ready than their predecessors to assume that the practice of Scots verse would continue to be kept up without a conscious determination on their part that it should be. Such an attitude implies some recognition of the danger (which had certainly become real) that it might not continue to be kept up. The one sure and certain way by which that might happen would be by the destruction of the Scottish community whose spoken language was the language of Scots poetry. The Industrial Revolution did virtually destroy the old Scottish community which is implied in the poetry of Ramsay, Fergusson and Burns.

9

Allan Ramsay's Scots Poems

Allan Ramsay's services in various ways to Scottish literature would require a long account if justice were to be
done to them all. As publisher and editor—although,
as we should think, a very bad editor—he did invaluable work
in re-establishing in the eighteenth century a Scottish literary
tradition, and thus helping to make possible Fergusson and
Burns. In purifying of their ruder elements the songs of the
Tea-Table Miscellany for the tea-table, he introduces into
them with the best intentions considerable impurity. They
read mostly as conventional eighteenth-century popular songs,
with here and there lines and even whole stanzas of genuine
folk-song persisting. There is nothing in Ramsay of the genius
in this respect of Burns. But in the *Miscellany* he initiated
experiments which that genius was to carry to fruition. As
editor and publisher of the *Evergreen* he resurrected part of
the older Scots poetry and popularized it, though at the
expense of doing it some injury. Ramsay was thus at any
rate sufficiently more conscious of the literary Scottish past
than others of his time to succeed in re-establishing a Scottish
tradition with its aid. His bookshop seems to have become the
centre of an Edinburgh cultivated circle—a place where there
could be that 'exchange of ideas' without which a literary
culture cannot become effective. Ramsay[1] was an unusually
active man of varied interests—he took a practical interest,

[1] His son (of the same name) is with Raeburn one of the two finest
Scottish painters of the eighteenth century.

for example, in painting and music in addition to literature—
and that he possessed great courage is shown by his attempt
to establish a theatre in the teeth of Presbyterian Edinburgh.
I am not concerned here, however, with Ramsay's services to
Scottish literature in ways other than as himself something of
a Scots poet, perhaps after all the directest way in which he is
related to his two successors of genius.

Ramsay's own achievement as a poet seems to me limited
to a modicum even of his Scots poems, which themselves form
only a proportion of all that he wrote in verse. His Scots
pastorals (he has been chiefly famous of course as the poet of
the *Gentle Shepherd*) cater for what was essentially an English
taste, even if that taste existed (or was created by Ramsay
himself) also in Scotland. An advantage which Ramsay's (and
Fergusson's) pastorals have over Gay's is that their 'rustic
dialect' assists for the townsman the atmosphere of a real
'rustic' world. Personally I have found Ramsay's *Fables*—
the Scots equivalent of Gay's *Fables*—much more amusing to
read than the faded *Gentle Shepherd*. 'Some of the following,'
he says in his advertisement to his *Fables and Tales*, 'are taken
from Messieurs la Fontaine and la Motte, whom I have en-
deavoured to make speak Scots with as much ease as I can.
. . . A man who has his mind furnished with such a stock of
good sense as may be had from these excellent Fables, which
have been approved of by ages, is proof against the insults of
all those mistaken notions which so much harass human life;
and what is life without serenity of mind?' They are at least
an attempt to re-establish contact in Scots with the literature
of Europe, and though they are of course very much less significant in almost every way than the *Fables* of Henryson,
they have gained something of neatness at least from the
French models. Prosaic though they are they do 'furnish', as
the product of Ramsay's maturer years, 'a stock of good sense'
with a sufficient proportion of quiet entertainment.

Ramsay's Horatianism (he did a good deal in the way of
translation and imitation of Horace), though it is again connected with an English fashion, seems to form almost the chief

part of what he found to say significantly in Scots verse. Unlike his pastoralism, I do not feel that it is merely Scotticized but that it has become in fact Scots. The following is from the third of the *Seven Familiar Epistles* that passed between him and Hamilton of Gilbertfield:

> Ne'er fash about your neist year's state,
> Nor with superior pow'rs debate,
> Nor cantrapes cast to ken your fate;
>   There's ills anew
> To cram our days, which soon grow late;
>   Let's live just now.
>
> When northern blasts the ocean snurl,
> And gars the heights and hows look gurl,
> Then left about the bumper whirl,
>   And toom the horn;
> Grip fast the hours which hasty hurl,
>   The morn's the morn.
>
> Thus to Leuconoe sang sweet Flaccus,
> Wha nane e'er thought a gillygacus;
> And why should we let whimsies bawk us,
>   When joy's in season,
> And thole sae aft the spleen to whauk us
>   Out of our reason?
>
> Tho' I were laird of tenscore acres,
> Nodding to jonks of hallen-shakers,
> Yet crush'd wi' humdrums, which the weaker's
>   Contentment ruins,
> I'd rather roost wi' causey-rakers,
>   And sup cauld sowens.

This kind of commentary on life seems a genuine characteristic because his verse there, and again in the following, is so satisfactory:

> The cauldripe carlies clog'd wi' care,
> Wha gathering gear gang hyt and gare,
> If ramm'd wi' red, they rant and rair,
>   Like mirthfu' men,

107

It soothly shows them they can spare
A rowth to spend.
What soger, when with wine he's bung,
Did e'er complain he had been dung,
Or of his toil, or empty spung?
Na, o'er his glass,
Nought but braw deeds employ his tongue
Or some sweet lass.

The most significant part of Ramsay's is the most thoroughly Scottish part—that is, the familiar epistles and the elegies in the mode of Robert Sempill's seventeenth-century *Habbie Simson, the Piper of Kilbarchan*. Ramsay could be thoroughly Scots in these modes because they were distinctively Scots modes. The epistles and elegies, unlike the pastorals, allow no feeling of something not quite assimilated. The strength of his idiom in the epistles and elegies is shown in its power to subjugate satisfactorily heroes and gods, make them human folk.

Sae some auld-gabbet poets tell,
Jove's nimble son and leckie snell
Made the first fiddle of a shell,
On which Apollo
With meikle pleasure play'd himsel'
Baith jig and solo.

(*Elegy on Patie Birnie.*)

That bang'ster billy, Caesar July,
Wha at Pharsalia wan the tooly,
Had better sped had he mair hooly
Scamper'd thro' life,
And 'midst his glories sheath'd his gooly
And kiss'd his wife.

(*Seven Familiar Epistles.*)

How fortunate Ramsay was in his idiom, which not merely saves him from prose but at times raises him to poetry, may be illustrated again by these stanzas from the *Elegy on Patie Birnie* (a famous fiddler):

When strangers landed, wow sae thrang,
Fuffin and peghing, he wad gang,
And crave their pardon that sae lang
He'd been a-coming;

108

Syne his bread-winner out he'd bang,
 And fa' to buming. . . .
How pleasant was't to see thee diddle
And dance sae finely to his fiddle,
With nose forgainst a lass's middle,
 And briskly brag,
With cutty steps to ding their striddle,
 And gar them fag.

That represents fairly the most valuable and vital part of what
Fergusson and Burns inherited directly from Ramsay.

10

Robert Fergusson

Fergusson, Allan Ramsay's successor, is an unmistakable poetic genius—a claim which could not be made for Ramsay, although it was the work of Ramsay as an editor and publisher, and as himself in his verse epistles and his elegies in the mode of *Habbie Simson* something of a Scots poet, that made practicable so late Fergusson's (and consequently Burns's) great poetic fulfilment. 'Fulfilment' may seem the wrong word to use of Fergusson's poetry. Fergusson died in a madhouse at the age of twenty-three, so that in one sense his poetry remains a fragmentary promise. But in another sense, together with that of Burns, it is a fulfilment of what had been preparing unobtrusively for at least two centuries.

It is necessary at first to distinguish between the various conventions that Fergusson inherited. He inherited a certain amount of conventionality of the kind that one cannot help feeling was an encumbrance to him however excellently he acquitted himself as a 'literary artist'. In his eclogues (*à mal mariée*, elegiac, etc.) he inherited Ramsay's pastoralism, a Scotticized version (the 'aiten reed') of the English pastoralism of Gay and others; but just one translation (Horace, Ode XI, Lib. I) connects him with Ramsay's Horatianism. Where his verse is weakest, if occasionally charming, is where it is related as a Scotticized variety to the eighteenth-century Spenser of English verse, as in the hybrid *Farmer's Ingle* (which in some ways anticipates the *Cottar's Saturday Night*), or, more often, the eighteenth-century Milton of *Lycidas, L'Allegro* and *Il Penseroso*; the latter combines easily with the pastoralism. Even *Auld Reekie*, one of Fergusson's best poems, weakens appreciably from the point where the eighteenth-century pastoral Milton becomes audible. But from Ramsay and his predecessors Fergusson inherited also living Scots verse conventions (the Scots verse epistle and elegy, and the mode of his *Hallow Fair* and *Leith Races*) that had been given a new lease of life; and his most significant and best work is an extension of these Scots conventions. If the first half and more of *Auld Reekie* may be said to be the Scots equivalent of anything English, it is of the Augustan verse of Pope and Swift which incorporates their most active actual interests.

It is impossible not to think of Fergusson as the predecessor of Burns. So much is Burns the fulfilment of Fergusson that it seems almost superfluous to attempt to distinguish them. Yet there seems good ground for the view that the fame of Burns has tended to deprive Fergusson of the attention he deserves and to obscure his peculiar merits. Fergusson of course has nothing like the fertile comic *flow* of Burns's Kilmarnock poems, nor is that flow to be found anywhere else in Scots. The language of Dunbar, though its vocabulary is, if possible, even richer than that of Burns, forms much less an irrepressible flow on. Yet Fergusson inherited from the people and the poets of the people the same magnificent language as Burns, and he transmitted it to Burns re-created, renewed in poetry of vivid life. In so far as Fergusson is different from Burns the difference is expressed by their individual use of the potentialities of the same inexhaustible language.

The best part of the poetry of Fergusson, that which is related to his most actual experience, is essentially a product of the Edinburgh of the eighteenth century. It is the product of a town community that was still distinctly rural in character and speech. Superficially this community was partially legal in aspect, and it received added picturesqueness and dash from the presence of soldiers at the Castle and a town guard, aspects that are reflected in the images of Fergusson's poetry;

but fundamentally its life was that of a small town community that was the focus of an extensive rural community.

> Tir'd o' the law, and a' its phrasis,
> The wylie writers, rich as Croesus,
> Hurl frae the town in hackney chaises
>   For country cheer.[1]

The poetry is, as the life was, fundamentally rustic, Bacchanal —if we think of barley instead of grapes. The barber of the satiric *Braid Claith* may here be selected as a representative figure of the comic observation of the men and manners of this community, which is characteristic of Fergusson's best poetry:

> On Sabbath-days the barber spark,
> Whan he has done wi' scrapin wark,
> Wi' siller broachie in his sark,
>   Gangs trigly, faith!
> Or to the Meadow, or the Park,
>   In gude Braid Claith.
>
> Weel might ye trow, to see them there,
> That they to shave your haffits bare,
> Or curl an' sleek a pickle hair,
>   Wou'd be right laith,
> Whan pacing wi' a gawsy air
>   In gude Braid Claith.

and through which it reaches to sure knowledge of the human heart—

> Braid Claith lends fouk an unco heese,
> Makes mony kail-worms butter-flies,

---

[1] *The Rising of the Session.* The rising and sitting of the Court of Session contributed to the rhythm of Edinburgh life. The impulse that carried the lawyers into the country at the rising of the Session is comparable to that which sends Chaucer's folk on pilgrimages. The Law and all its phrases suddenly appears empty of meaning to those impelled to seek again their fathers' farms in a return to nature—or to rural quiet (the Horatian note). The dram-house and coffee room are deserted. But the Sitting of the Session (a companion poem has this title) in November is equally an occasion for rejoicing. The town resumes its full life; the Edinburgh community gathers in for the winter.

> Gies mony a doctor his degrees
>> For little skaith:
> In short, you may be what you please
>> Wi' gude Braid Claith.

> For thof ye had as wise a snout on
> As Shakespeare or Sir Isaac Newton,
> Your judgement fouk wou'd hae a doubt on,
>> I'll tak my aith,
> Till they cou'd see ye wi' a suit on
>> O' gude Braid Claith.

Clothes thus absurdly metamorphose a man and decide what people think of him. But the satire is not ungenial. The spirit of holiday is in the rhythm, and in the spectacle of the little barber dressed in his Sunday best, promenading up and down in the human fair.

It may be noted as significant that this poetry registers explicitly in more than one place vigorous local *resistance* to Italian and French influences.

> Fiddlers, your pins in temper fix
> And roset weel your fiddle-sticks,
> But banish vile Italian tricks
>> From out your quorum;
> Nor *fortes* wi' *pianos* mix,
>> Gie's *Tulloch Gorum*.

It is a changed attitude. The poetry is evidently the product of a community which—vigorous though it is—feels itself in some degree *threatened* from outside. No longer feeling that it belongs to a great European community, from which it obtains nourishment, it withdraws into itself from influences which it instinctively feels to be hostile to its still vigorous identity. It was fortunate in having such resources to fall back on behind its local defences. A number of phrases from *Caller Water* will show that the poetry is still vigorous enough to incorporate into its 'local' life allusions to the ancient mythologies and poetry.

> Whan father Adie first pat spade in
> The bonny yeard of antient Eden. . . .

> The fuddlin' Bardies now-a-days
> Rin maukin-mad in Bacchus' praise,
> And limp and stoiter thro' their lays
>   Anacreontic,
> While each his sea of wine displays
>   As big's the Pontic. . . .
> The fairest then might die a maid,
> And Cupid quit his shooting trade. . . .

Elsewhere the idiom is still capable of mastering Euclid (*Elegy on the late Professor of Mathematics in the University of St. Andrews*),

> He could, by Euclid, prove lang syne
> A ganging point compos'd a line,

and it even digests some law Latin. That the eighteenth-century rationalistic studies were among the influences creating schisms within the mind of the community itself, the following clash presented in the concreteness of a 'character' (that of John, the late porter at St. Andrews University) may perhaps suggest:

> 'I hae nae meikle skill, quo' he,
> 'In what you ca' philosophy;
> 'It tells that baith the earth and sea
>   'Rin round about;
> 'Either the Bible tells a lie,
>   'Or you're a' out.
>
> 'It's i' the psalms o' David writ,
> 'That this wide warld ne'er sho'd flit,
> 'But on the waters coshly sit
>   'Fu' steeve and lasting;
> 'An' was na he a head o' wit
>   'At sic contesting!'

The satiric idiom depreciates both viewpoints.

The strength and originality of Fergusson's poetic imagination may be observed at its best in the Edinburgh night-scene in *Auld Reekie*.

> Whan feet in dirty gutters plash,
> And fouk to wale their fitstaps fash;

114

At night the macaroni drunk,
In pools or gutters aftimes sunk;
Hegh! what a fright he now appears,
Whan he his corpse dejected rears!
Look at that head, and think if there
The pomet slaister'd up his hair!
The cheeks observe, where now cou'd shine
The scancing glories o' carmine?
Ah, legs! in vain the silk-worm there
Display'd to view her eident care;
For stink, instead of perfumes, grow,
And clarty odours fragrant flow.

The richness of this magnificent comic poetry arises from its unusual combinations of images and sharp contrasts. The corpse upreared from the gutter—the *gutter* associations combined with the *corpse* associations (for surely that 'corpse' carried the associations of *dead* body)—are contrasted with 'the pomet slaister'd up his hair', 'slaister'd' however itself suggesting something messy, and with 'the scancing glories o' carmine', 'carmine' introducing at the same time with the glories the unpleasant associations of rouge. So, through the superb juxtaposition of 'legs . . . the silk-worm's care', the contrasts culminate sharply in those compressed in the last phrases—'stink instead of perfumes' and 'clarty odours fragrant'. That Fergusson's poetic imagination was essentially a comic imagination, fantastically enlarging its object, may be illustrated again from the *Election*. This poem describes one of those important public occasions which change into occasions for conviviality and end as indecorously as they have begun pompously. There is first the morning scene when John dresses. The coat that has been laid aside all the year is fetched out, and multitudes of moths and insects are dislodged from it.

The coat ben-by i' the kist-nook,
　That's been this towmonth swarmin,
Is brought yence mair thereout to look,
　To fleg awa' the vermin:
Menzies o' moths an' flaes are shook,
　An' i' the floor they howder.

115

That this was the direction in which Fergusson's genius lay, a comic imagination at work on what interested it in the actual life that lay to hand, may be brought out again by a comparison between the poem *On Seeing a Butterfly in the Street* (though not one of Fergusson's most characteristic poems) and the companion pieces *To the Bee* and *To the Goudspink*. These latter are pieces in the eighteenth century pastoral meditative mode (considerably influenced by the Milton of *L'Allegro* and *Il Penseroso*) and they remain on the whole little divergent from the run of these charming conventional exercises. *On Seeing a Butterfly in the Street*, on the other hand, because of the introduction of the contrasting actual associations implied in *in the Street* has a considerable dash of Fergusson's characteristic witty life.

> Daft gowk, in macaroni dress,
> Are ye come here to shew your face,
> Bowden wi' pride o' simmer gloss,
> To cast a dash at Reikie's Cross;
> And glowr at mony twa-legg'd creature
> Flees braw by art, tho' worms by nature?

11

Burns

There are certain elementary distinctions to be stressed before a just estimate of Burns becomes possible. His Scottish verse must first of all be isolated not only from his own English verse (which is so obviously bad that it may at once be dismissed as such) but from English verse. It has no connections with English verse at any point, so that to consider it as a 'reaction' to the English eighteenth-century manner or, along with Wordsworth, the beginning of the nineteenth is (and has been) to breed confusions. What it is connected with is the Scottish vernacular verse which for at least two centuries precedes it and of which it is for all practical purposes the culmination. I take *Christis Kirk on the Green* and *Peblis to the Play* as strictly the earliest examples of this tradition. The native elements which have again begun to develop independently in these pieces are present in the verse of Dunbar and Henryson. But the verse of Dunbar and Henryson is not independent in this sense. It has something in common with the rest of medieval verse. It is Scottish and European. *Christis Kirk on the Green, Peblis to the Play,* the vernacular verse of the Sempills, Ramsay, Fergusson and Burns, is, on the other hand, Scottish and independent.

This latter tradition, if narrow, is correspondingly definite. *Christis Kirk, Peblis to the Play,* Fergusson's *Leith Races* and *Hallow Fair*, Burns's *Holy Fair* and *Hallowe'en* are in kind identical. So also are the verse epistles which start with those of Ramsay and Hamilton of Gilbertfield and end with those of

117

Burns. *Habbie Simson, the Piper of Kilbarchan,* is the first of
a series of which the burlesque elegies of Burns are the end.
It was probably a positive advantage to Burns that he was
compelled to work within these narrowly defined limits. It was
a condition probably of his success. But the three years of
poetic productivity at Mossgiel, which resulted in the Kilmarnock volume, were, it seems, sufficient practically to ex-
haust the possibilities. It is difficult to see what else was left
him to do, if he was not simply to repeat himself, except turn
for the remainder of his life to the songs.

Watson's Choice Collections had made *Christis Kirk, Peblis
to the Play,* Montgomerie's *Cherry and the Slae* and other poems
generally accessible to the eighteenth century; and Ramsay
had 'modernized' even Dunbar and Henryson for his *Evergreen.* But Burns inherited the past of Scottish vernacular
verse essentially, and particularly, through the vernacular
verse of Ramsay and Fergusson, his immediate predecessors.
He invents nothing himself; he sums up the vernacular verse,
and brings it to a climax.

The past, in a wider sense, was still vital in the life and
speech with which he was in daily contact, that is, in the life
and speech which were also his own. This folk speech cannot
be separated from the folk life, of centuries of which it is the
product. It is a speech which is itself almost poetry, in that it
is close down to the life of sensation and saturated with the
concrete wisdom of folk experience connected with the soil.
The marvellous vitality which is characteristic of Burns's
poetry belongs not merely to Burns but to the language. (See
the last verse of *Epistle to Davie.*) In a sense the language, at
its fullest expression, *is* Burns. To borrow a phrase Mr. Leavis
has used of Shakespeare, Burns 'incarnates' the Scottish vernacular. This is his strength. The language throws up phrases
of the type,

> blethering, blustering, drunken blellum,
> fleechin', flethrin',
> huff'd an' cuff'd an' disrespeckit,

> delvers, ditchers and sic cattle,
> vines an' wines an' drucken Bacchus,

which result from no surface manipulation of it. These develop
into 'flyting' passages:

> May gravels round his blather wrench
> An' gouts torment him, inch by inch,
> What twists his gruntle wi' a glunch . . .

The use made of the language there must be distinguished
from the more deliberate comic collocation of vv. 20–3, *Death
and Doctor Hornbook*. Generally the language bears its own
more immediate fruition—phrases 'as fully flavoured as a nut
or apple'.[1]

> He draws a bonnie silken purse
> As lang's my tail, where, thro' the steeks,
> The yellow letter'd Geordie keeks.

The only thing comparable to Burns's poetry is the flowering
of Elizabethan folk speech in the Falstaff passages of Shakespeare. That speech belongs to a phase when 'the town' was
still essentially part of the country; as the Edinburgh of
Fergusson and Ramsay was. It is a speech as far as possible
removed from the bloodless speech, and uprooted, bloodless
lives, that exist in the tea-shops, dance-halls, cinemas, offices,
factories, municipal 'workers' houses', bungalows, of our
sprawling modern Suburbia. Burns's poetry represents what
in Scotland, as in England, has been destroyed. Nothing like
it is possible now, because the conditions that make a vernacular verse of any kind possible no longer exist.

Burns's failure to write anything better than inferior Pope,
Gray and verse of the Thomson and Beattie and Shenstone
kind when he writes English verse is therefore not without its
significance. English was alien to him, no intimate part of his
life as was his own speech, so that when he attempts to break
the bounds of the narrow vernacular verse tradition by writing

[1] Synge, Preface to the *Playboy*.

English verse (more especially in the years following the Kilmarnock volume), he invariably loses contact with the source of his own power. Writing to Thomson (the Song-Collector), he himself says:

> These English songs gravel me to death. I have not the command of the language that I have of my native tongue. In fact I think my ideas are more barren in English than in Scottish.

This has been the case of other Scotsmen, even Scott. *Proud Maisie* and one or two other poems in the Scottish ballad manner are Scott's contribution to poetry. Fortunately it was still possible for Burns to be a poet of the vernacular, and in general he knew, with profound intuitive knowledge, what he was doing. (See vv. 9–12, *Epistle to Lapraik.*)

Burns never writes bombast in the vernacular—*bravura*, but not bombast. His knowledge of (and by virtue of) the vernacular is too intimate. There is present in the vernacular a shrewdness, a traditional folk sense, which would in any case have kept him right. This profound good sense which is characteristic of Burns as a vernacular poet, and uncharacteristic of him as an English poet, is a different thing from the eighteenth-century English 'good sense'. It has nothing to do with 'decorum'. But its effect is somewhat similar in that Burns is essentially (the fact has been obscured) a great comic, and satiric, poet.

The satires of David Lindsay (no doubt because directed against the abuses of Rome) had enjoyed a continued popularity among the Scottish folk surpassed only by the Bible. Two centuries of theological controversy had made of the Scottish peasant if not a theologian at least a controversialist, acutely aware of the satiric, as well as the vituperative, possibilities of the vernacular. Burns inherited a Scottish satiric tradition therefore, both through the vernacular itself and through literary practice in the vernacular, as far back, in fact, as medieval church satire. But (it must be observed) there is a more considerable element of satire in Burns's verse than there is in the vernacular verse from which (as verse) it derives. The line from *Christis Kirk* to Fergusson is characteristically comic but not satiric. Any account of Burns's satire must therefore start rather from a consideration of how he utilized the possibilities present in his medium. I shall endeavour to isolate for this purpose two of the 'forces' behind certain of Burns's satiric effects.

The phrase 'gospel kail'[1] exhibits in concentrated form one of these. It is essentially a combination of the same startling kind as

> A bracelet of bright hair about the bone.[2]
> Lilies that fester.[3]
> Christ the tiger.[4]

The associations of 'gospel' are forced into unexpected combination with those of 'kail', the tension (resulting from their mutual opposition) being extreme. But Burns's phrase differs both in itself and in the use—or one of the uses—it is put to in its context. The result of the combination in its case is partially destructive in that 'gospel' must be equated to 'kail'. The energy thus released is what is absorbed into the satire. Further, the associations of 'kail' are 'local' and, as such, contrast with the 'wider' associations of 'gospel'. The vernacular is as much a matter of idiom as of vocabulary, in that only part of the vocabulary is (as it had become) 'local'. Burns characteristically plays this 'local' part of his vocabulary against the other part:

> There, at Vienna or Versailles,
> He rives his father's auld entails;
> Or by Madrid he takes the rout,
> To thrum guitars an' fecht wi' nowt.[5]

The world of Vienna and Versailles, because balanced against the more immediate 'local' world of

> He rives his father's auld entails,

suffers satiric depreciation; as, more explicitly, in the preceding lines of the same passage:

---

[1] *The Ordination.*   [2] Donne.   [3] Shakespeare.
[4] Eliot.   [5] *The Twa Dogs.*

> Or maybe, in a frolic daft,
> To Hague or Calais taks a waft,
> To make a tour, an' tak a whirl,
> To learn *bon ton*, an' see the worl'.

It is the 'local' world, on the contrary, which suffers the satiric depreciation in *Holy Willie's Prayer* (the finest of Burns's satires):

> An' when we chasten'd him therefor,
> Thou kens how he bred sic a splore
> As set the warld in a roar
>   O' laughin' at us;
> Curse thou his basket and his store,
>   Kail and potatoes.

Burns appreciates its littleness in relation to the God whom Holy Willie (who is of it) familiarly addresses. But he does not appreciate its littleness as a citizen of Europe. On the contrary, this 'local' world, such as it is, is Burns's own world, and its solidity in comparison with any other is in general at the basis of his satire and (as I hope to indicate later) of much of his comedy too.

Another of the 'forces' behind certain of Burns's satiric effects is exaggeration. The satire takes effect at the point at which the exaggeration becomes distortion.

> Or purse-proud, big wi' cent per cent
> An' muckle wame . . .[1]

Broad caricature was inherent in Burns's medium, in that— being possessed of the vigour of folk speech—it admitted of this magnificent coarsening:

> Some gapin', glowerin' country laird
>   May warsle for your favour;
> May claw his lug, and straik his beard,
>   And host up some palaver.[2]

Another of the lady's possible suitors is contemptuously dismissed in the equally exaggerated diminutiveness of the line:

> Some mim-mou'd pouther'd priestie.

---

[1] *Second Epistle to Lapraik.*   [2] *Willie Chalmers.*

The exaggerated gestures of the preacher are themselves
exaggerated—

> Hear how he clears the points o' faith
> Wi' rattlin' an' wi' thumpin'!
> Now meekly calm, now wild in wrath,
> He's stampin' an' he's jumpin'![1]

—to the point of it being suggested that the preacher dances
a jig in the pulpit—involved in the fun of the Fair. 'But now
the Lord's ain trumpet touts.'

Satire is, of course, found in Burns in varying degrees and
in association with a variety of qualities. *Holy Willie's Prayer*
is parody, in which the eloquence contributes to the satiric
effect. The postscript to the *Epistle to William Simpson* is a
flight of nonsense, a satiric fantasia. The *Holy Fair* differs from
the poems from which it derives in being satiric at all. Its effect
is a complicated one—in the particular way its title suggests.
It is satiric, in general, in combining the humorous associations
of a fair with those of a church, but there is also other satire
in it:

> When by the plate we set our nose,
>   Weel heaped up wi' hapence,
> A greedy glow'r Black Bonnet throws,
>   An' we maun draw our tippence.

and

> But, faith! the birkie wants a manse. . . .

Death's account of the patients killed off by the amateurish-
ness of Dr. Hornbook is, perhaps, less satiric than simply witty,
as in the surprise at the end of the stave:

> A countra laird had ta'en the batts,
> Or some curmurring in his guts,
> His only son for Hornbook sets,
>   An' pays him well:
> The lad, for twa guid gimmer-pets,
>   Was laird himsel'.

It is, in fact, not always easy to disentangle the satire.

> I rhyme for fun.[2]

[1] *Holy Fair.*   [2] *Epistle to James Smith.*

Satire in Burns is never very radically dissociated from the
Satyric. A quality of its anthropological origins adheres to
both his satiric and comic poetry. It is rooted in the rustic
festivals, the saturnalia which persisted among the peasantry
in spite of Calvinism. Much of it suggests a Dionysiac rout and
revel, an intoxication, a dance. The description perhaps applies
most simply to *Hallowe'en*, in which the exhilaration is sustained to the end by a swift succession of surprises. But Burns's
greatest pieces are all of essentially the same nature—*The
Jolly Beggars*, his most representative and, as even the highly
serious Arnold thought, his greatest performance, and *Tam o'
Shanter*, a later and more studied performance. (*The Cottar's
Saturday Night* is of course an obvious fake.) These, and perhaps the bulk of his finest comedy, are essentially extravaganza.
The comedy tends to farce—of various kinds. The following
passage from *Tam o' Shanter* (in which *tour de force* the amazing
transitions from passage to passage are rather carefully stage-
managed, though only possible at all, of course, by the nature
of his idiom) is comic melodrama at the point of farce:

> By this time he was cross the ford,
> Where in the snaw the chapman smoor'd;
> And past the birks and meikle stane,
> Where drunken Charlie brak's neck-bane;
> And thro' the whins, and by the cairn,
> Where hunters fand the murder'd bairn;
> And near the thorn, aboon the well,
> Where Mungo's mither hang'd hersel'.

There is an abandon suggested in Burns's verse everywhere
which has a strangely invigorating effect. Calvinistic decorum
is outraged:

> Ye are sae grave, nae doubt ye're wise;
> Nae ferly tho' ye do despise
> The hairum-scairum, ram-stam boys,
>   The rattlin' squad:
> I see you upward cast your eyes—
>   Ye ken the road.[1]

[1] *Epistle to James Smith.*

124

('nae doubt ye're wise'—'Ye ken the road'—spring from an ironic habit of speech which was not merely personal). Not that Calvinism is not something to be understood and perhaps respected. But what is reasserted in Burns's poetry (in the very rhythm of it, I mean) is a human normality older than Calvinism. To fall back on terms I have already used, a catharsis takes place from which an essential sanity—and contentment—results. The rhythm of Burns's poetry is never essentially depressed, not even, I feel, in the vernacular passage at the beginning of *The Vision*, where it comes near it:

> Had I to guid advice but harkit,
> I might, by this, ha'e led a market,
> Or strutted in a bank, and clarkit
>   My cash-account;
> While here, half-mad, half-fed, half-sarkit,
>   Is a' th' amount.

But in general his world is a self-contained—and satisfying—one. I have described it as a 'local' world. But in one sense it is not comprehended by other worlds. In the phrase,

> Eden's bonnie yard,[1]

'Eden' has been annexed by 'bonnie yard'. The meagre fragments which have come down through the vernacular verse from other verse—Phoebus, Pegasus, Parnassus—have likewise become part of it, and do not suggest an externality. The occasional stray personifications have lost contact with the older personification habit (and are not, of course, Gray and Collins). That of Fun,[2] at the beginning of *Holy Fair*, has ceased to be recognizable as a personification:

> Wi' bonnet aff, quoth I, 'Sweet lass,
>   I think ye seem to ken me;
> I'm sure I've seen that bonnie face,
>   But yet I canna name ye.'

The Beast Fable survives, perhaps, into *The Twa Dogs*, the *Poor Mailie* poems, and others, but it has become another thing—part of this familiar 'local' world:

---

[1] *Address to the De'il.*   [2] It derives from Fergusson's *Mirth.*

> But ay keep mind to moop an' mell
> Wi' sheep o' credit like thysel',

—which is the world of familiar 'local' conversation.

Death and the De'il belonged, already, to folk conversation. *The Address to the De'il* and the macabre caricature of Death in *Death and Dr. Hornbook*, and the drunken home-farer's moonlit conversation with it, depend for their comic effect on being 'conversation' pieces in this 'familiar' idiom and vocabulary:

> 'Guid-een,' quo' I: 'Friend! hae ye been mawin'
> When ither folk are busy sawin'?'
> It seem'd to mak a kind o' stan',
>   But naething spak;
> At length says I, 'Friend, w'are ye gaun?
>   Will ye go back?'

This 'familiarity' is the 'devastating familiarity' with which (someone has remarked) in the political satire Fox, Pitt, the Prince of Wales,

> That vile doup-skelper Emperor Joseph,

and the Scottish Representatives (in the *Earnest Cry and Prayer*) are depreciated.

Burns's verse is, therefore, related on the one hand (I continue to postpone consideration of the Songs) to conversation. It has, particularly in the Epistles and Addresses, the informality, and flexibility, of such.

> Sae I've begun to scrawl, but whether
> In rhyme, or prose, or baith tegither,
> Or some hotch-potch that's rightly neither,
>   Let time mak proof;
> But I shall scribble down some blether
>   Just clean aff-loof.[1]

The inflexions of the speaking voice are extremely subtly reproduced in the poem *To a Louse* (the masterpiece, I am inclined to think, among his shorter comic pieces). The movement of the poem, and the changes in the movement, correspond with the movements of the creature and suggest these:

[1] *Second Epistle to Lapraik.*

Na, faith ye yet! ye'll no be right
Till ye've got on it,

and so to the shift of attention in

O Jenny, dinna toss your head . . .

The various changes in the key (if I may use this analogy here) are another index of the poem's dramatic vitality. The 'flyting' manner of the second verse, for example, modulates into the brobdingnagian exaggerations of the third. A number of Burns's poems (*Holy Willie's Prayer*, for one, and even, perhaps, a majority of the Songs) are explicit dramatizations.

But to say that Burns's verse is related to conversation is only a half-truth. His verse is verse, a heightened thing, which is the result of several relations. He regarded himself (when writing in the vernacular) as a 'rhymster', and his 'rhyming', as such, is indeed so amazing that it demands consideration for itself.

> For me, I'm on Parnassus' brink,
> Rivin' the words to gar them clink;
> Whyles dazed wi' love, whyles dazed wi' drink.[1]

This is hardly an adequate account. Burns's rhyming springs, rather, from a heightened consciousness of words as such (not so dissimilar from that from which the Elizabethan pun sprang), so that words become associated together (as also in the assonantal phrases I have already cited) through similarity of sound rather than of abstract 'meaning'.

Metrically, and otherwise, Burns's verse (I wish finally to suggest) is affected by Scottish folk-dance. It seems to me to bear something of the same kind of relation to the folk-dance as is borne by much Jacobean verse to Jacobean Stage-Play. This is certainly true of the vernacular Songs. Words, tune and dance are, in these, essentially one. The tunes to which Burns composed new, or rehandled old, words were as often as not reels and strathspeys. The dance affects the Songs through these tunes and (as I have suggested in a previous paragraph) the rest of his verse in less tangible ways.

[1] *Second Epistle to Davie.*

I have postponed consideration of the Songs not merely because they were the labour of the last ten years of his life, but because I think they can best be understood in relation to the Kilmarnock poems, which form the centre of his work. Burns, of course, worked on several different kinds of song, and these must be carefully distinguished. The songs he found in the Song-Books were very miscellaneous, and there are only a few fragments of folk-song even in Ramsay's *Tea-Table Miscellany*. He writes one or two 'passable'[1] eighteenth-century English popular humorous songs (after the manner of those of the *Beggar's Opera*, a selection of which are in the *Miscellany*). But his 'literary' English songs are as bad as the rest of his English verse. The 'sensibility' cult (we are told that he carried about the *Man of Feeling* in his pocket) breaks in upon them, whereas it scarcely affects the vernacular songs. It is essential, therefore, that the vernacular songs should be considered separately, and along with the rest of his vernacular verse. They are the consummation of Scottish folk-song.

Burns's methods of composition of these have elsewhere been admirably gone into.[2] It was an immense labour, part creative, part critical, as many of his letters witness:

> ... *excellence* in the profession is the fruit of industry, labour, attention, and pains.

The qualities of these folk-songs are essentially those of the rest of his vernacular poetry—speeded up to the dance, till they become an ecstasy:

> Comin' through the rye, poor body,
> Comin' through the rye,
> She draiglet a' her petticoatie,
> Comin' through the rye.
> Jenny's a' wat, poor body;
> Jenny's seldom dry;
> She draiglet a' her petticoatie,
> Comin' through the rye. . . .

[1] His own description.
[2] Recently, by W. A. Edwards in his chapter on 'The Traditional Artist as Borrower' in his *Plagiarism* (Minority Press).

We're a' dry wi' drinkin' o't,
  We're a' dry wi' drinkin' o't;
The minister kiss'd the fiddler's wife,
  An' could na preach for thinkin' o't. . . .

She has an ee, she has but ane,
  The cat has twa the very colour;
Five rusty teeth, forbye a stump,
  A clapper tongue wad deave a miller;
A whiskin beard about her mou',
Her nose and chin they threaten ither;
  Such a wife as Willie had,
  I wadna gie a button for her. . . .

The weary pund, the weary pund,
  The weary pund o' tow;
I think my wife will end her life
  Before she spin her tow.

There sat a bottle in a bole,
  Beyond the ingle lowe,
And aye she took the tither souk
  To drouk the stowrie tow. . . .

The cardin' o't, the spinnin' o't;
  The warpin' o't, the winnin' o't;
When ilka ell cost me a groat,
  The tailor staw the linin' o't. . . .

Green grow the rashes, O,
  Green grow the rashes, O;
The sweetest hours that e'er I spend,
  Are spent amang the lasses, O!
There's nought but care on ev'ry han',
  In ev'ry hour that passes, O;
What signifies the life o' man,
  An' twere na for the lasses, O.

I here shift the emphasis from *O, my luve's like a red, red rose,
Of a' the airts, Bonnie Doon, Go, fetch to me a pint o' wine,* and
Mary Morrison not because I wish finally to deny that these
are the summit of achievement, but because I wish to bring
them out of relation with nineteenth-century lyric poetry and

into relation with the comic background of the rest of Burns's vernacular work. It seems to me that only thus can a right appreciation of them be achieved. The world of Burns's vernacular poetry is a single complete world and, essentially, a world of comedy.[1]

[1] This essay is the earliest in this book. It was first published in *Scrutiny* in 1934.

12

The Scottish Ballads

As we have them in the Collections, the Scottish Ballads are poems chiefly of the eighteenth century. That they are quite different from other poems of that century may at first occasion surprise, but has its explanation. On the other hand it has been denied (by the primitivists) that they are poems of that century at all. It has been argued that there is no reason to suppose they did not come into being centuries earlier than the century in which they were written down. It has also been observed that a good deal of the 'material' used is 'medieval'. But a poem and the language it is in are one and the same. Translated, it either becomes a new poem or ceases to be a poem at all. It is sufficient therefore to point to the language the ballads are in, which in most cases is at the point of development it was in the eighteenth century. (This is not merely a matter of language, but of sensibility. The ballads taken down after the beginning of the nineteenth century show a distinct modification of sensibility.) Certainly the ballads are traditional. But so also is every poem—in its owndegree.[1]

I have isolated the Scottish Ballads from the other ballads in Child's Collection for the purposes of this consideration. Child includes several: *Judas, St. Stephen and King Herod,* which belong with medieval verse. *Robyn and Gandelyn* is fifteenth century, and the finer of the Robin Hood Ballads also

[1] I would now (1961) say that I got the emphasis wrong in this paragraph. The Ballads *are* a residue from medieval poetry—therefore, with a *long* oral tradition behind them.

are rather earlier than the Scottish Ballads. The broadsheets that fluttered across the English country from the printing presses of 'the town' are more nearly contemporaneous with the Scottish Ballads. Scotland seems to have suffered less than England from the broadsheet contagion, being at that time less exposed, though nowadays newspapers, in Scotland as in England, have long since superseded ballads and broadsheets both. There are comparatively few Scottish Ballads in Percy's *Reliques*. But it was in Scotland that the Collectors of the eighteenth century found their finest poems.

The Scottish Ballads and the English Ballads are not wholly distinct from each other, but both are distinct from 'literary' English verse. The simultaneous existence of two distinct types of verse points to the simultaneous existence of two distinct traditions. But that is no reason for supposing, as has been done, that the oral tradition (represented by the ballads of the Collections) and the 'literary' tradition were distinct to begin with, since an examination of the ballads themselves, their metre,[1] their conventions, shows them to be not medieval verse certainly, but a development, a 'popular'[2] development, from medieval verse. They were the verse which entertained the largely unlettered 'people', and they possess in themselves a life distinct and apart both from the 'literary' verse they were contemporaneous with and from the medieval verse they are a development from.

The Scottish Ballads therefore are, as every poem is, new and at the same time old. They are late (later, I think, than has been held) in that they belong mostly to the eighteenth century, but late also in that they bear on themselves the mark of a long ancestry. They are stiff with a Poetic Diction. To illustrate this Poetic Diction with an exhaustive list of phrases

[1] Since metre of this kind was not introduced into English verse (from the French) until the fourteenth century, the ballads must have undergone surprising structural, as well as linguistic, changes, if one adopts the 'primitivist' view.

[2] 'Most of these ballads', says Bishop Percy of his *Reliques*, 'are of great simplicity, and seem to have been merely written [*sic*] for the people.'

132

—*yellow hair, cherry cheeks, lily-white, rose-red, clay-cauld*—
would be superfluous; the ballads themselves are the composite illustration of it; any analysis of the ballads is necessarily
an analysis of it. Its strength is that it is to a considerable
extent a stylization of popular speech. It is simple: it is
sensuous: and it retains something of the passion of popular
speech. Its most evident 'limitation' as an artistic medium is
perhaps its intractability to the expression of subtle shades of
perception, its ready formation of simple, and at moments
brutally effective, contrasts:

> And clear, clear was her yellow hair
> Whereon the red blood dreeps,

not only in colour:

> Shool'd the mools on his yellow hair.

When therefore the late eighteenth century began looking for
a poetry which should be 'simple, sensuous, and passionate',
it certainly found such in the ballads. What fascinated the late
century were these 'natural' qualities and not merely that
here was a Poetic Diction different from the prevailing Poetic
Diction and therefore 'fresh'. Bishop Percy in his introduction
to his *Reliques* (1765) is still apologetic, but he indicates clearly
enough what he, and his contemporaries, supposed were the
merits of the ballads.

> In a polished age, like the present, I am sensible that many of
> these reliques of antiquity will require great allowances to be
> made for them. Yet have they, for the most part, a pleasing sim
> plicity, and many artless graces, which in the opinion of no mean
> critics[1] have been thought to compensate for the want of higher
> beauties, and, if they do not dazzle the imagination, are fre
> quently found to interest the heart.

The description is to a certain extent just. We can all of us
recall lines in the ballads which affect us suddenly and sharply
(to express it more strongly than the Bishop) with an apparent
utmost economy of means. Yet once the stylization of the

[1] He names 'Mr. Addison, Mr. Dryden and the witty Lord Dorset' in a
footnote.

diction, especially in certain of the Scottish Ballads, is perceived the impression is more generally one of 'conventionality'. It will be sufficient to refer the reader to the finer of the *Twa Sisters* (*Binnorie*) variations. But the precise degree of conventional richness of one couplet from one ballad—

> The bride cam tripping down the stair[1]
> Wi' the scales o' red gowd on her hair,

—cannot of course be appreciated unless one remembers the recurrences in other ballads of 'brides', ladies who 'cam tripping down the stair', 'red gowd' and adorned 'hair'.

This Poetic Diction is built into a Rhetoric—partly by means of repetitions.[2] The *Gil Brenton* (*Cospatrick*), the *Cruel Brother* and the *Babylon* variations come first to my mind as exemplifying it. What it indicates is the adaptation of speech to something outside itself, to declamation or to song. This also imposes upon it a certain rigidity which arrests any development from it, such as there was in Elizabethan dramatic verse from its earliest rhetorical 'simplicity' to its later close-down-to-speech complexity. But what in the ballads is lost in simplification is gained in effectiveness of dramatic presentation:

> 'What news, what news?' said young Hind Horn;
> 'No news, no news,' said the old beggar man,
>
> 'No news,' said the beggar, 'No news at a',
> But there is a wedding in the king's ha'.'[3]

What the repetition does is to increase the expectancy. This is resolved into a surprise. 'A conversation' seems to be reproduced in what seems a hard, unyielding medium, but with (as also, and more especially, in *Lamkin*) quite astonishingly effective results. The ballad dialogue is both itself stylized and an

---

[1] *Hind Horn.*

[2] But the importance of the refrain to the ballads as we have them has been over-emphasized, I think.

[3] Whatever the origins of the ballads, ballad recital and composition were, at least to some extent, a collaborative activity. It is possible to see in the ballads, as they were sung or recited, a social and popular dramatic art that flourished among the Scottish people.

integral part of the stylization. 'All imaginative art', writes Yeats (in his remarkable essay *Certain Noble Plays of Japan*), 'remains at a distance, and this distance once chosen must be firmly held against a pushing world. . . . The arts which interest me, while seeming to separate from the world and us a group of figures, images, symbols, enable us to pass for a few moments into a deep of the mind that had hitherto been too subtle for our habitation' . . . seem, in fact, 'to recede from us into some more powerful life. . . .' The ballads are more than the beginnings of such an art.

When the eighteenth century found the ballads artistically 'rude' and 'unpolished' it may have been simply that the variations are for the most part very fragmentary, so that anything like a completely formed poem in the literary sense is rare. The ballads are sets of variations, fragmentary indeed, but in the extremely conventionalized medium I have spoken of. It is in this sense they are 'impersonal' apart altogether from their anonymity as to authorship.

Not that this medium itself remains constant. Even the Scottish Ballads, considered as a group by themselves, break up into lesser groups as soon as one looks at them closely enough. *Hughie the Graeme, Dick o' the Cow, Jamie Telfer, Jock o' the Side, Kinmont Willie,* for example, form a group possessing robust characteristics of its own, considerably apart from what I have taken to be the central group. But these lesser groups retain a vital relation with each other and with the whole, which evidences a homogeneous community, in vital contact also with its neighbours but not dependent on imported stuff.

The mere existence of this ballad poetry among the largely unlettered Scottish 'people' in the eighteenth century is evidence also of the existence then of a popular taste that there is no equivalent of now among the lettered 'people' either in Scotland or in England.[1] The contemporary popular taste as

[1] Mr. Robert Graves is interested in the 'ballads' that came into existence among the British troops during the war of 1914, but these have little intrinsic or permanent value, as he would agree.

represented by the contemporary popular entertainment (popular fiction, popular films, jazz music) is of a very much lower order. There is now such a gap between it and the literary tradition that it is difficult to know how long the literary tradition itself, deprived of sustenance from beneath, can persist.

But more particular evidence of the quality of popular taste a generation or two ago is provided by a comparison between the variations of any ballad (such as was recently made by Professor Gerould). Between the eight variations of the two opening lines of the *Unquiet Grave* (which Professor Gerould sets down) there is indeed very little to choose. This is the case also with an astonishingly large proportion of the ballad variations. Whether they were always the result of forgetfulness or not (it is very doubtful) they exhibit an astonishingly high degree of artistic competence to have been so widespread. Whoever was responsible for them could substitute lines as good for the lines which were either forgotten or not. They exhibit in practice a popular taste acquired, quite unconsciously, through long familiarity with ballads. My reason for doubting whether the variations arose simply from the necessity for filling up gaps in memory, rather than from some deeper necessity, may become clear from a comparison between two passages from two variations of the *Cruel Mother*:

CHILD B. As she was going to the church,
    She saw a sweet babe in the porch.

O sweet babe, and thou were mine,
    I wad cleed thee in the silk so fine.

O mother dear, when I was thine,
    You did na prove to me sae kind.

CHILD C. She has howked a hole baith deep and wide,
    She has put them in baith side by side.

She has covered them oer wi a marble stane
    Thinking she would gang maiden hame.

As she was walking by her father's castle wa,
She saw twa pretty babes playing at the ba.

O bonnie babes, gin ye were mine,
I would dress you up in satin fine.

O cruel mother, we were thine . . .

These variations are in fact two independent poems. There is here a difference of vision.

This suggests also the nature of what, I think, one learns to look for in the Scottish Ballads. When the fragments belonging to the group are set together (not that one supposes they were ever anything else than fragmentary) portions of the outlines of a pattern within that of the conventionalized medium become discernible. What these form the very fragmentary revelation of is a folk-mythology. It is, I wish tentatively to suggest, the central thing in the Scottish Ballads, from which a complete understanding of them must proceed. It is here:

> She's gane into the Jew's garden
> Where the grass grew lang and green:
> She powd an apple red and white
> To wyle the young thing in.[1]

It is also here:

> I'll show you where the white lilies grow
> On the banks of Italie.

And later in the same poem:[2]

> 'O what hills are yon, yon pleasant hills,
> That the sun shines sweetly on?'
> 'O yon are the hills of heaven,' he said,
> 'Where you will never won.'

> 'O whaten a mountain is yon,' she said,
> 'All so dreary wi frost and snow?'
> 'O yon is the mountain of hell,' he said,
> 'Where you and I will go.'

[1] *Hugh of Lincoln.*
[2] *The Demon Lover.* (*The Carpenter's Wife.*)

and it is, wizened, here:

> She's turned me into an ugly worm
> And gard me toddle about the tree.[1]

It is a symbolism which is unmistakable wherever it occurs—
the green garden, the apple, the braid, braid road across the
lily leven (*Thomas the Rhymer*) or down by yon sunny fell
(*Queen of Elflan's Nourice*), the rose broken from the tree
(*Tam Lin*), the nut broken from the tree (*Hind Etin*), the
place 'at the foot of our Lord's knee' 'set about wi gilly-
flowers' where women go who die in child-birth (*Sweet William's
Ghost*). I find what corresponds with it in Bunyan, whose work
is the expression of a folk-mythology which is not merely
derivative from the Authorized Version. But I seem to find
the same quality of vision, individualized, in Blake.

It is at this point that it becomes necessary to stress the
fundamental difference between the Scottish Ballads and the
Romantic Poetry of the nineteenth century (with which work
Blake is also, I think, wrongly associated). That poetry took
over for its own purposes a quantity of what may be described
as the 'machinery' of the ballads. Its Poetic Diction is derived,
through Coleridge and *La Belle Dame Sans Merci*, almost as
much from that of the ballads (chiefly because of their apparent 'picturesque' medievalism) as from Spenser and Milton.
But this Poetic Diction is cut off from the vigour—

> She stickit him like a swine

—of the popular speech which the Poetic Diction of the ballads
is to a considerable extent a stylization of. Correspondingly
there is nothing in common between the vital, if very fragmentary, vision of the Scottish Ballads, and the insubstantial
dream of nineteenth-century poetry.

The ballad art, like other art, seems 'to separate from the
world and us a group of figures, images, symbols' and thereby
'enables us to pass . . . into a deep of the mind'. It is difficult
to resist the conclusion that nineteenth-century 'appreciation'

[1] *Alison Gross.*

subtly externalized (and sentimentalized) the significance of these 'figures, images, symbols', even those which most appealed to it:

> And he saw neither sun nor moon
> But he heard the roaring of the sea.[1]

has a 'definite' significance in its context.

> 'Get dancers here to dance', she said,
>   'And minstrels for to play,
> For here's my young son, Florentine,
>   Come here wi me to stay . . .'

> For naething coud the companie do,
>   Nor naething coud they say,
> But they saw a flock o' pretty birds
>   That took their bride away.[2]

There is more than a nursery-tale significance in, for example, the birds—that is to say, in *Cow-me-doo* as well as in the *Twa Corbies*; rather, there is the significance there often is, latent, in a nursery-tale which has been folk-tale.

If the symbolism of which I have spoken is kept in mind, the other images too assume, in varying degrees, a symbolical value in relation to it. The images of finery, for example, particularly of dress, which are so frequent in the Scottish Ballads, are then recognized to possess a symbolical value as profound as in Bunyan ('. . . he that is clad in Silk and Velvet'). That finery is associated with folly, pride and death. It is Vanity.

> Fair Margaret was a rich ladye
>   The king's cousin was she;
> Fair Margaret was a rich ladye
>   As vain as vain could be.

> She ward her wealth on the gay cleedin
>   That comes frae yont the sea,
> She spent her time frae morning till night
>   Adorning her fair bodye.

[1] *Thomas the Rhymer.*   [2] *Earl of Mar's Daughter.*

> Ae night she sate in her stately ha,
> Kaimin her yellow hair . . .[1]

This religious sense is behind the peculiar satiric element (a fierce exultant derision almost) in the lines:

> O our Scots Nobles were richt laith
> To weet their cork-heild schoone;
> Bot lang owre a the play wer playd,
> Thair hats they swam aboone.

> O lang, lang may their ladies sit,
> Wi thair fans into their hand,
> Or ere they se Sir Patrick Spence
> Cam sailing to the land.

> O lang, lang may the ladies stand
> Wi thair gold kems in their hair,
> Waiting for their ain deir lords,
> For they'll se thame na mair.[2]

And this religious sense is present also, pityingly and wonderingly, in

> But she put on the glistering gold
> To shine through Edinburgh town,

in its *Marie Hamilton* context—a poem which seems to me charged with this religious sense.

The ballads are concerned, it is true, almost entirely with the circle of the life of the body, with birth, instinctive action, death (often violent death), and the decay of the body. Again, they present on the one hand (as W. P. Ker and others noted) images of a princely grandeur erected out of earth, and on the other hand, its counterpart, the earthiness of death and decay. These images are contrasted and associated, if not explicitly, by their mutual presence. The total effect is thus sombre. It has been customary to speak of the 'paganism' of the Scottish Ballads. I suppose I mean the same thing, but I should prefer to describe them (keeping in mind the symbolism I have

[1] *Proud Lady Margaret.*
[2] Version from Percy's *Reliques.*

spoken of) as, in a profound sense, 'religious'.[1] They embody, in any case, very fragmentarily indeed, but with startling immediacy, a tragic vision of human life which sprang, apparently, from the imagination of the 'folk'.

[1] The beautiful English specifically religious folk-poems (*St. Stephen and King Herod*, *The Cherry-Tree Carol*, for example) require to be appreciated separately and along with the Miracle Plays.

13

Nineteenth-century Scotland in Allegory

It was doubtless the vogue of idyllic 'kailyard' fiction that provoked George Douglas to the prosaic 'realism' of *The House with the Green Shutters*. But what appears to sustain it is an almost terrifying dissatisfaction with the Scotland itself he had known. The book not merely implies a criticism of certain other books that in any case are no longer read—that it killed the 'kailyard' type of fiction is its historical importance—it implies a radical *social criticism* amounting to an indictment, and it is as such that it may have its present importance; for while I would not admit it to the highest rank as a work of the novelist's art—to the rank, that is to say, of *Wuthering Heights*, the novel with which one immediately compares it in one's mind—its value *as a work of art* seems to me to depend on the value of the social criticism it implies. As a 'tragedy' detached from these implications it seems to me at once 'conventional' as if its author were striving to conform to some exterior idea of 'tragedy' which he supposes himself perhaps to have got from the Greeks. Expectation is preferred to surprise according to the best models; the 'bodies' are thought of as filling the role of the 'chorus', and so on. The scenes of pity (not weakly indulged) and terror—horror rather—towards the end would appear to justify it as a 'tragedy' in this conventional sense. But the source of the power the book undoubtedly has, can, it seems to me, be shown to exist in reality in the terrible nature of its social criticism.

142

The novel presents a number of different individuals—centring in the members of the Gourlay family—in the setting of a small local community—that of Barbie—which is in a late phase of disintegration. Whether or not Barbie was characteristic of the Scotland of the nineteenth century must be left to the social historian to confirm; in any case 'Barbie' has, I think, a general application. 'Barbie has been a decaying burgh for thirty years', we are told explicitly in the beginning of the second chapter. To call Barbie a 'community' is indeed to extend the meaning of the word; it has ceased to be an 'organic community'; there is no longer a fruitful co-operation between its members. The 'bodies' who represent the last of the local public opinion and should have been, without necessarily knowing it, the guiding and controlling centre of the community are—destructive worms bred out of the decaying organism—idly malicious gossipers and back-biters. 'The Bend o' the Brae was the favourite stance of the bodies: here they forgathered every day to pass judgment on the town's affairs.' This is a specimen of their conversation:

'Losh,' said Sandy Toddle, 'yonder's the Free Kirk minister going past the Cross! Where'll *he* be off till at this hour of the day? He's not often up so soon.' . . .

'What road'th he taking?' lisped Deacon Allardyce, craning past Brodie's big shoulder to get a look.

'He's stoppit to speak to Widow Wallace. What will he be saying to *her*?'

'She's a greedy bodie that Mrs. Wallace: I wouldna wonder but she's speiring him for baw-bees.'

'Will he take the Skeighan Road, I wonder?'

'Or the Fechars?'

'He's a great man for gathering gowans and other sic trash. He's maybe for a dander up the burn juist. They say he's a great botanical man.'

'Ay,' said Brodie, 'paidling in a burn's the ploy for him. He's a weanly gowk.' . . .

'I'm demmed if he hasn't taken the Skeighan Road!' said Sandy Toddle, who had kept his eye on the minister. . . .

'The Skeighan Road! the Skeighan Road! Who'll he be going to see in that airt? Will it be Templandmuir?'

143

'Gosh, it canna be Templandmuir; he was there no later than yestreen!'

'Here's a man coming down the brae!' announced Johnny Coe, in a solemn voice, as if a man 'coming down the brae' was something unusual. In a moment every head was turned to the hill.

'What's yon he's carrying on his shoulder?' pondered Brodie.

'It looks like a boax,' said the Provost slowly, bending every effort of eye and mind to discover what it really was. . . .

(Chapter V.)

The quality of their 'judgments' may be appreciated in the following:

Drucken Wabster and Brown the ragman came round the corner, staggering.

'Young Gourlay's drunk!' blurted Wabster—and reeled himself as he spoke.

'Is he a wee fou?' said the Deacon eagerly.

'Wee be damned,' said Wabster. 'He's as fou as the Baltic Sea! If you wait here, you'll be sure to see him! He'll be round the corner directly.'

'De-ar me, is he so bad as that?' said the ex-Provost, raising his hands in solemn reprobation. He raised his eyes to heaven at the same time, as if it pained them to look on a world that endured the burden of a young Gourlay. 'In broad daylight, too!' he sighed. 'De-ar me, has he come to this?' . . .

'I kenned young Gourlay was on the fuddle when I saw him swinging off this morning in his greatcoat,' cried Sandy Toddle. 'There was debauch in the flaps o' the tails o't.'

'Man, have you noticed that too!' cried another eagerly. 'He's aye warst wi' the coat on!' . . .

'We may as well wait and see young Gourlay going by,' said the ex-Provost. 'He'll likely be a sad spectacle.'

'Ith auld Gourlay on the thtreet the nicht?' cried the Deacon eagerly. 'I wonder will he thee the youngster afore he gets hame! Eh, man'—he bent his knees with staring delight—'eh, man, if they would only meet forenenst uth! Hoo!' . . .

(Chapter XXI.)

Yet the 'bodies' are in a sense what has become of the past, and as traditional figures are significant, as well as richly comic. The Deacon, and for example (at the beginning of Chapter XXII) David Aird, the City bounder about to return

144

to the City after finding Barbie 'too quiet for his tastes'
('Thank God, we'll soon be in civilisation'), form a significant
comic contrast; but it is the Deacon alone who is satirically
aware of the other.

The laird and the minister, who would have been shown as
somewhere near the centre had the novel been written in the
eighteenth century, are little more here than dots on the
periphery. The laird has sunk into identity with the surrounding commonality. He is proud to have an evening's 'sederunt'
with old Gourlay—at least until he marries a miller's daughter
(of a different kind from Tennyson's—'Her voice went with
the skirl of an east wind through the rat-riddled mansion of
the Hallidays'). The minister, the Rev. Mr. Struthers, is an
exceptionally stupid peasant—he has taken ten years to get
into the Church and has had a reverence for the university
ever since; though what he reverences is mainly the wonder of
its administrative machinery. The scene (Chapter XX) in
which he congratulates the young prize-winner ('Ability to
write is a splendid thing for the Church') is one of the richest
in comedy. As for the schoolmaster he 'rarely leaves' his
studying of the theory of Political Economy—

> 'Ay,' he said dryly, 'there's a wheen gey cuddies in Barbie!'
> and he went to his stuffy little room to study *The Wealth of
> Nations*.

—a study which being disconnected from what is happening
around him in Barbie is socially barren.

Here then is a society without aristocratic or ecclesiastical
or pedagogic leadership or guidance. Presbyterianism itself
is no longer substantial; it persists vestigially as some of its
effects. It has left behind a certain hardness and bitterness
in character and conversation, an absence of sap and sweet-
ness:

> 'It's a fine morning, Mr. Gourlay.'
> 'There's naething wrong with the morning,' grunted Gourlay,
> as if there was something wrong with the Deacon.

The Provost's 'Huts, man, dinna sweer sae muckle!' is a kind of unconscious reminiscence of the grave reproofs of elders. The ironic technique of the traditional speech goes on functioning out of relation to its proper object.

> 'What's that you're burying your nose in now?' and if she faltered 'It's the Bible,' 'Hi,' he would laugh, 'you're turning godly in your auld age. Weel, I'm no saying but it's time!'

The skeleton of Presbyterianism can seem terribly forbidding:

> Heavy Biblical pictures, in frames of gleaming black like the splinters of a hearse, were hung against a dark ground.

There being no longer a community holding together and controlling its members, the sheer individual, Gourlay, of peasant stock, stupid, but of tremendous dourness and brute force of 'character' thrusts upward. He builds the House with the Green Shutters on the top of the hill. It represents his attempt at self-sufficiency—the house apart. 'It is his character in stone and lime,' and it dominates the town. Since the public opinion—as represented by the 'bodies'—is impotent to control him, the malevolence of the 'bodies' grows monstrous against him. With shakes of the head they judge Gourlay's house as Vanity and 'Pride that *will* have a downcome.' But the traditional judgment loses most of its force from being made the vehicle of their petty personal spite.

Gourlay maintains his position till the advent of another individual, Wilson, who, although a native of Barbie, has been —significantly—*away* for an interval of years.

> In his appearance there was an air of dirty and pretentious well-to-do-ness. It was not shabby gentility. It was like the gross attempt to dress of your well-to-do publican.

He introduces the familiar modern business methods. (They are described in some detail in Chapters X, XI and XIII.)

> Now the shops of Barbie (the drunken man's shop and the dirty man's shop always excepted, of course) had usually been lowbrowed little places with faded black scrolls above the door, on which you might read in dim gilt letters (or it might be white)

'Licens'd To Sell Tea & Tobacco.'

When you mounted two steps and opened the door, a bell of some kind went in the interior, and an old woman in a mutch, with big specs slipping down her nose, would come up a step from a dim little room behind, and wiping her sunken mouth with her apron—she had just left her tea—would say, 'What's your wull the day, Sir?' and if you said your 'wull' was tobacco, she would answer, 'Ou, Sir, I dinna sell ocht now but the tape and the sweeties.' And then you went away, sadly.

With the exception of the dirty man's shop, and the drunken man's shop, that kind of shop was the Barbie kind of shop. But Wilson changed all that.

Gourlay, although a type of the individualism which both followed from and contributed to the break-up of the Scottish community, is himself thoroughly Scottish. Wilson is no longer Scottish, but nondescript modern commercialism and 'progress'.

The downfall of the Gourlay family gains in significance from being a particular instance of a more general downfall. The house of Gourlay looks well enough from the outside and in its yard—

A cock pigeon strutted round, puffing his gleaming breast and *rooketty-cooing* in the sun. Large, clear drops fell slowly from the spout of a wooden pump, and splashed upon a flat stone.

—but inside it is in filthy disorder, for Gourlay has a sluttish wife, and his son and daughter are ailing in mind and in body; the fruit of Gourlay's pride is internally rotten. Gourlay's attempt to found a self-contained house and family dominating Barbie has to come to nothing sooner or later in any case, for young Gourlay, his son and heir, is a 'weakling'. Yet we are shown clearly enough that brought up in more favourable conditions there is sufficient in young Gourlay to have brought forth some fruit. He is gifted with a wealth of sensuous perceptiveness represented in passages of a prose that in this respect reminds one oddly of Katherine Mansfield's.

But as young Gourlay's schoolmaster and, later, his professor perceive, he is without the mind and character to use this wealth so as to make it something other than an incubus. The difficulties of the sensitive adolescent Scot are dealt with in a way that seems to anticipate what *The Portrait of the Artist as a Young Man* does for the Irish adolescent. In the case of the adolescent Scot there is almost no tradition, no sympathetic understanding community to guide him; prematurely born, he is subjected only to the brutal will of his father and the weak indulgence of his mother. Not that the novelist attempts to invoke our sympathy for him. He is dealt with as unsympathetically as almost everyone else in the book. It is part of the bracing effect of the book that it is almost wholly unsympathetic. Douglas is a stringent moralist, scrupulously searching out moral failure. As a moralist he is perhaps too *explicit* for a novelist. But as that is not a fault of much modern work, it is almost to be welcomed here as a sign of health than otherwise. A moral preoccupation in the finest sense of 'moral' may be held to be an essential for a novelist, perhaps for any artist.

Young Gourlay is sent to Edinburgh University to be made into a minister. ' "Eh, but it's a grand thing a gude education! You may rise to be a minister," his mother had said when he was sent to the secondary school. "It's a' he's fit for," his father had growled.' Old Gourlay has no illusions as to the sacred profession. He wants to put his son into it as an expedient for saving the falling fortunes of his house. At this point, then, the focus is shifted from a small rural burgh to the very capital of Scotland itself and to what might be expected to be the centre of its cultural life, Edinburgh University. Young Gourlay at Edinburgh is partly a test of what Edinburgh and its university had to offer. It might not have been too much to expect that here if anywhere the youth might have found the conditions, lacking in Barbie, favourable for the multiplication of his single talent. Douglas's picture of Edinburgh and its university is no flattering one. Edinburgh offers the 'weakling' only too much encouragement in his suicidal tendency to whisky addiction. The lecture rooms, where as one of a mob of rowdy students he has his sole opportunity of confronting his professor, are twice presented in the condition of a bear-garden. 'Auld Tam', the Scots professor,

148

is indeed a figure to be reckoned with. He is representative of the Scots professor of the days before Scots professors were mostly Englishmen from Oxford and Cambridge, and he possesses powers of mind and character (he quells the unruly students with the humorous acerbity of his tongue) which we are bound to respect. Being also a representative of the tradition of philosophy and abstract speculation, he is amusingly inadequate when attempting to deal with something so concrete and particular as *Macbeth*. What effective culture there might seem still to be in Edinburgh is represented by the Allan circle. There seems to me a serious weakness betrayed by Douglas in his portrayal of this circle (Chapter XVII). The novelist seems to accept it almost at its own valuation. If, as appears, Douglas intends it to be regarded as really 'brilliant', he does not succeed in convincingly representing it as such. Could it have been that Douglas, in general so without illusions, was himself impressed by the sort of thing represented by Tarmillan, the most 'brilliant' apparently of the Allan circle? The superficial, even vulgar, cleverness of the wit of Tarmillan's conversation is something sadly inferior to the corresponding thing there is reason to believe there was in the Edinburgh of the eighteenth century. 'The Howff'—the pub which night after night lures young Gourlay to it out of his dismal room and away from his uncongenial books—represents what had become of the tradition to which at an earlier phase Burns's poetry belongs. It is a survival from the older Scotland; as is the groset-fair and such an episode (and such a vocabulary) as the following:

> They roared and sang till it was a perfect affront to God's day, and frae sidie to sidie they swung till the splash-brods were shreighing on the wheels. At a quick turn o' the road they wintled owre; and there they were, sitting on their doups in the atoms o' the gig, and glowering frae them!

But for young Gourlay 'the Howff' is no longer an expression of the robust enjoyment of bucolic life; it is merely a refuge to shrink into from the terrors that assail his sensitivity. The novel ends, inevitably, on the notes of Insanity, Disease,

Murder, Suicide. The tendency is not only in young Gourlay; it is in the whole of the society of which the novel is a grim representation. This seems to me the nature of the tragedy of the novel, by virtue of which it may prove permanently applicable.

What is to be one's final word on the book as a contribution to literature? The quality of a novel is, of course, that of its prose both locally and as a cumulative organic whole. The passages extracted above give a fair idea of Douglas's prose at its working best. The passage about the thunderstorm at young Gourlay's birth (Chapter VI) might be extracted, together with its echo later (Chapter XIV) that so terrified the truant boy, if the comparison with *Wuthering Heights* is to be insisted on. But Douglas's prose is not always so good. At times it appears insufficiently controlled—emotions 'seethe' and 'boil'—and on the other hand, while frequently exhibiting a rich particularity, it occasionally drops into something like the journalist being 'literary'. That the book was Douglas's first (and only) novel may explain its immaturities, as its astonishing power may seem to have offered great promise of future achievement; but it is not easy to believe that the life of a journalist in London would have qualified him to write a greater Scottish novel; and in any case considerations of what he might have done ought not to deflect the critical judgment on what he did do. That Douglas's prose should so consistently preclude sympathy is of course its unusual strength. If that unsympathy could have been converted into a purely artistic detachment and sustained as such, the novel would have been a great work of art. Unfortunately, as an examination of its prose at once confirms, the unsympathy is not always that of detached and serenely poised art, but seems at times to proceed from an unresolved personal animus. There is not space to extract the opening passage of the book for examination, but I may perhaps refer to it. It is Douglas's prose at its best, but even here the 'silly' of 'The silly *tee-hee* echoed up the street' is perhaps a sign of this insecurity. There may be some justice also in the common dismissal of the book as 'merely depressing'. Douglas does indeed refer to certain positives in at least one place—

> To bring a beaten and degraded look into a man's face . . . is an outrage on the decency of life, an offence to natural religion, a violation of the human sanctities.

—but these positives, though referred to, are nowhere strongly and positively realized in the book. If they had been it would perhaps have been a wiser, because more complete, book. Nevertheless, if not a great novel, it is, because of the clarity of the social criticism it implies, a very remarkable one.

14

The Present and C. M. Grieve

There are some reasons why this chapter might well have been the first. The present grows out of the past, and is only rightly to be understood in relation to the past; but equally the past only exists for us in and through our present, and only has present value in so far as it can be brought to bear on the problems of the present. For that reason all observations (unless they are to be merely academic) must begin and end with a concern for the present.

In order the better to measure the immediate present it will be an aid to hold in mind Dunbar as representative of the great phase of Scots; and to assist this, some recapitulation may first of all be permitted. (1) Dunbar is an accomplished metrist. To say this is to say something more important than is commonly intended. It is to imply his maturity in the sense that he is at the outcome—almost, but not quite, pushed outside his material—rather than at the beginning of a growth of poetic tradition. His arrangements of words have behind them a weight of traditional sanction. (2) His forms and conventions, modified as they were by his particular language, were European, the expression of a European consciousness, in the sense that they were common to the poets of Medieval Europe modified by the language—English, French, Italian and Church Latin—of each. (3) The particular language he wrote in was not French, Italian, Latin (nor on the other hand Gaelic); it was Scots. The second and third of these commonplaces imply a poetry that is medieval and European and at the same time

152

Scots. It is in this sense that Burns is provincial in comparison with Dunbar. It is not merely that Dunbar is a 'court poet', Burns the culmination of a 'popular' tradition. The Scotland of Burns no longer formed part of a European background. Today Mr. C. M. Grieve (Hugh McDiarmid) attempting to write a new Scots poetry is a forlorn and isolated figure, the European background having vanished, and Scotland with it. When therefore Grieve reiterated in his early days 'Not Burns —Dunbar!' no doubt his instinct guided him right. There is, it seems, a better reason for wishing to go back to Dunbar than the negative one that it is necessary to get away from Burns.

On the other hand, it should not be surprising that, however much Grieve may have wanted to get back to Dunbar, there is little evidence in his verse—and this after all is the ultimate test—that he has succeeded. 'Dunbar,' said Grieve, 'is singularly modern.' Modern in the sense that every poet capable of being realized afresh as significant Dunbar certainly is, or might be. It is in order that he may be felt to be 'modern' in this sense that it is necessary to emphasize that he is 'medieval' and that his connections with the poets of the Renaissance are comparatively few and slender,[1] and with poets later than the Renaissance non-existent.

Dunbar's achievement in the poems which are the core of his work is his combination of formalism with a closeness to speech. It is on this speech norm that his range, the ease of his transitions, and much else, depends. To write in Scots a poetry that is based on living speech (as the major part of Dunbar is), or even to write a Scots poetry that is based on a language of immediate literary practice (as is *The Goldyn Targe*), is no longer possible. There cannot be a Scottish poetry in the fullest sense unless there is in the fullest sense a Scottish speech.

[1] Mr. Allen Tate once suggested a connection between Dunbar and Donne's Satires through Sackville's *Induction*. There is indeed a resemblance since all three start from a medieval sense of human depravity and the vanity of earthly things, but that only serves to emphasize the differences between them.

What survives of such a speech among what survives of the peasantry is in its last stages and is even something its speakers have learned to be half-ashamed of. That is why there has been no Scottish literature (and indeed no literature in Scotland of any kind) since the eighteenth century.

When a language is destroyed it may be taken for granted that it is not only a language, it is a distinctive traditional life that has been destroyed, and with it all forms of the traditional art that springs from that life. There is little that is positively Scottish in the life of the modern cities, Glasgow, Edinburgh, or that distinguishes them from other cities of the modern world. The daily routine of the townspeople in factory, office and shop, the distractions provided for their leisure, are not distinctive. The country—much of it has of course been blotted out by the nondescript industrial areas—is penetrated by the motoring roads and has ceased to possess its own life apart from the towns. The country people are learning to share by means of bus and wireless the town-distractions. In their turn the cities overflow into the country in motor-cars on fine days and make of it their recreation ground. The 'life' the country witnesses on these days is a life alien to it, imposed upon it, disfiguring it.

There can be no literature unless there is further not merely a reading-public, but a *discriminating* reading-public, however small—such as existed in Scotland in the fifteenth century and again in the eighteenth. The evidence that in the fifteenth century—the century in which the universities of St. Andrews, Glasgow and Aberdeen had their origins in the medieval Catholic Church—there existed such a cultivated public and that its culture was both European and Scottish, is the poetry of Henryson, Dunbar, Douglas. It may or may not have had its immediate centre in the court—Henryson is no court poet, and Dunbar, who is even more various than Henryson, is a court poet and a poet of several other kinds—but at any rate it was something that was definitely there. The Edinburgh of the eighteenth century held in juxtaposition a poet so Scottish as Robert Fergusson and an eighteenth-century European in

David Hume. Even so late as the beginning of the nineteenth century there were the Edinburgh reviews. But today? The answer to the question why modern Scotland is essentially indifferent not only to Scots literature but to literature, would be very much the same as the answer to the question why the modern world is indifferent to literature. The same forces operate throughout the modern world.

The problem is how to recreate, or find some equivalent for, the tradition, or traditions, which have been destroyed. In the circumstances, the efforts of Grieve to recreate the literary tradition seem almost superhuman. So many names later became associated with the Scottish Literary Movement, initiated by Grieve in sincerity, that it became difficult to distinguish it from a publicity ramp. Many names were associated, if not quite similarly, with the Irish Literary Movement. There remain from that the positive achievements of Synge and Yeats. The fully Irish achievement of Synge was evidently still possible at that time in Ireland. Synge stylized Irish peasant speech that was still spoken. But if a poetry anything like so magnificently vital as that of the later Yeats, even if it were not so Scottish as that of Yeats is Irish, were being composed in Scotland, it would be more than justifiable to talk of literature, even if not in the fullest sense Scottish literature, in Scotland again. One finds oneself forced back upon the work of Grieve.

The weakness of such of Grieve's work as is in his 'Synthetic Scots' can at once be traced back to the fact that he himself does not speak 'Synthetic Scots', nor does anyone else. His medium is not a spoken medium. It remains at least doubtful whether anyone, even with Grieve's gifts, is qualified to accomplish much by starting so far back as first to create, or recreate, the language in which his poetry must be written. It has to be remembered, however, that so great has been the rate of change that the childhood of such men as Grieve and his friend, the composer F. G. Scott, was probably much more Scottish than their adult life now is. Secondly, it has to be remembered that Grieve is resurrecting words which are

155

embedded in what might be called his own racial past, endeavouring to find new powers of life in them, and to enrich the
present with them. But some of the English poems in his *Second
Hymn to Lenin* volume are *at least* as good as anything Grieve
has written in Scots. The equivalent could not be said of
Burns.

Grieve's problem included not only a problem of language
but also a problem of finding poetic modes he could make use
of. His failure to find such modes, or to persist in the development of such as he found, is one cause of the dissipation of his
powers. He does not in actual fact (in spite of what he wrote
of the necessity for doing so) begin from Dunbar but (in
Sangshaw) from the folk-ballad. The little that is in the Scottish folk-ballad mode is almost the only successful portion of
the *Drunk Man Looks at the Thistle*:

> O wha's the bride that cairries the bunch
> O' thistles blinterin' white?
> Her cuckold bridegroom little dreids
> What he sall ken this nicht.
>
> For closer than gudeman can come
> And closer to'r than hersel',
> Wha didna need her maidenheid
> Has wrocht his purpose fell.
>
> O wha's been here afore me, lass,
> And hoo did he get in?
> —*A man that deed or I was born
> This evil thing has din.*
>
> And left, as it were, on a corpse
> Your maidenheid to me?
> —*Nae lass, gudeman, sin' Time began
> 'S hed ony mair to gi'e.*
>
> *But I can gi'e ye kindness, lad,
> And a pair o' willin' hands
> And you sall ha'e my briests like stars,
> My limbs like willow wands.*

156

And on my lips ye'll heed nae mair
And in my hair forget,
The seed o' a' the men that in
My virgin womb ha'e met.

Millions o' wimmen bring forth in pain
Millions o' bairns that are no' worth ha'en.

Wull ever a wumman be big again
Wi's muckle's a Christ? Yech, there's nae sayin',

Gin that's the best that you ha'e comin',
Fegs but I'm sorry for you, wumman!

Yet a'e thing's certain—Your faith is great.
Whatever happens, you'll no' be blate! . . .

Mary lay in jizzen
As it were claith o' gowd,
But it's in orra duds
Ilka ither bairntime's row'd.

Christ had never toothick,
Christ was never seeck,
But Man's a fiky bairn
Wi' bellythraw, ripples, and worm-i'-the-cheek! . . .

There are three poems in the passage, but each is a modification, an individualized use, of a Scottish folk-ballad mode.
This (except possibly for some passages of satire on Burns
Clubs and St. Andrew's Night Dinners) seems to me to represent almost all of value that has come out of Grieve's really
admirable attempt to write a new Scots poetry. The attempt
(forming the bulk of Grieve's verse of this phase) to intellec-
tualize Scots poetry (this may have been what he meant by
going beyond Burns to Dunbar) seems to me unsuccessful so
far in spite of the attendant strength of his physiological
imagery. In *Circumjack Cirencrastus* the passage of adaptation
of Rilke (Rilke must have been unknown in Scotland in the
year Grieve's adaptation was made) stands out for its technical subtlety. The impact of the poetry of Rilke has acted as

a condenser to give a temporary form to the formlessness. But already this passage is in English. The only passages of interest in Scots in *Circumjack Cirencrastus* are the personal passages on his bitter experiences of the underworld which is modern journalism. But of the volume *Second Hymn to Lenin and Other Poems* (1935) I should be prepared to hazard the opinion that Grieve has at last really found himself. The best poems in this volume *resemble* certain occasional aspects of Blake and also of the Shelley of the *Mask of Anarchy* (compare their use of the political broadsheet technique), particularly in an anger finding direct, naïve expression. This particular naïveté is a much more difficult achievement than may at first appear. It marks the attainment of a difficult sincerity. It is the sign (unless I am mistaken) of an intellectual and spiritual distinction. In so far as there is any *influence* perceptible it is possibly that of the Yeats of some of the poems of the *Green Helmet, Responsibilities, The Wild Swans at Coole* phase, though Grieve is without Yeats's complexity. But the voice is quite individual.

> There is a monstrous din of the sterile who contribute nothing
> To the great end in view, and the future fumbles,
> A bad birth, not like the child in that gracious home
> Heard in the quietness turning in its mother's womb,
> A strategic mind already, seeking the best way
> To present himself to life, and at last, resolved,
> Springing into history quivering like a fish,

I would refer the reader especially to *Folly, In the Children's Hospital, Another Epitaph on an Army of Mercenaries, Like Achilles and Priam, In the Slaughterhouse, The Salmon Leap, The End of Usury, The Two Parents, Reflections in an Ironworks*. But these poems are in English. What they gain by being by Grieve and perhaps by being, in so far as they are, Scottish, may be judged by comparison with the work of the much publicized group of Public School Communist poets there has been in England; the difference is primarily in the fundamental sincerity of Grieve's poems. The *Second Hymn to Lenin*—the only poem in Scots in the volume—seems to me to have the distinction of being (I would not say an entirely satisfactory poem) the only really *contemporary* poem in Scots for many generations.

I have confined myself to a tentative and, perhaps, premature—as it must certainly seem severe—literary judgment on Grieve's verse. I have risked it only because I felt it must be attempted by someone, and this whole book has been, in a sense, an effort to qualify myself to make a contemporary judgment. As I look through again such of Grieve's work in prose and verse as is available to me, I am struck with admiration for the unusual powers of mind and spirit they display, though at every turn thwarted and frustrated. Partly his dissatisfaction and discontent is with an environment relentlessly hostile to the reality of art.

. . . but the better-off citizenry of Edinburgh still respect professional men almost as much as big business men; poets and writers however are another matter. It is not even a question of keeping them in their proper places; they have no place. . . .

Dundee Art Gallery is a byword. Public money has been wasted on worthless pictures in vicious taste and atrocious pictures of ex-Lord Provosts and other public men form a large part of the collection. It is noteworthy that although Dundee has long been the centre of a struggling colony of Scottish artists—men like Stewart Carmichael, Walter Grieve, David Foggie and others—they have got practically no civic encouragement, which has been lavished almost entirely on fashionable artists from the South, like Philip de Lazlo. . . .

It is by no accident that in the Shetlands, in Scotland, in England and elsewhere, there is an almost complete divorce between political and practical affairs, on the one hand, and poetry, philosophy and scholarship on the other, and that public life is in the hands of men with whom no creative artist worth a rap would waste a moment's time in associating. The hideous distress, barbarism, and hopelessness of our life are due to this divorce—to this appalling confusion of values—to all these worthy citizens of ours who would regard it as 'ballyhoo' to be told that social and economic regeneration depends very largely on sound cultural standards and that no country can have a decent economic and social order which has not good tastes in arts and letters and adequately pursues its own true creative spirit.

He turns and turns like a caged tiger. But through all his inconsistencies there is a consistency of direction—a devotion, a concentration of all his powers to the end in view. In this he shows a quite extraordinary strength of character. For no one is more aware of his tragedy than Grieve.

If Grieve finally succeeds in solving his problem it will not be only his own problem he will have solved; he will have helped towards solving the problem of any other Scotsman who may aspire to poetry (or, for that matter, prose). To return to the example of Yeats. There is a good deal that is Irish in Yeats's English. It may be assumed that, similarly, if a modern writer of Scottish antecedents succeeded in writing poetry of the English he spoke there would prove to be a good deal that is Scottish in that English. In so far as a writer is 'Scottish', his 'Scottishness', even if he is himself not conscious of it, will show itself in what he writes. This is certainly true of the writer who possesses the honesty of genius, and since there can be no literature without this kind of honesty it is true of anything that may justifiably be called literature. There was no more distinctively 'Scottish' writer than Dunbar. But it is unlikely that it was his primary and deliberate aim to be so. If the centre of interest, even in the case of a writer of Scottish antecedents, is in a literature that shall be 'Scottish', then the interest is not wholly that of a creative artist in his work. A difficult problem of sincerity arises. As soon as a writer attempts to be something other than himself in what he writes there is a dissociation which is bound to show itself in a certain falsity in the writing. This is true of a Scottish writer who attempts in his writing to be other than Scottish. But it is equally true of a writer of Scottish antecedents, whose ordinary conversation is in what is approximately English and whose share in intellectual discussion is also and more necessarily 'English' and who yet deliberately and self-consciously attempts to be 'Scottish' in some of the things he writes as distinct from nearly everything he says. I try here to suggest some of the dangers. I would not be taken as saying that if one's antecedents are Scottish it should not be one's endeavour to be as conscious of those antecedents as possible. On the contrary, it has been my ultimate contention that what has gone wrong is that most Scottish people have lost consciousness both of their Scottish antecedents and of their European antecedents, and of their Scottish antecedents and their European antecedents as having once been one. But to be deliberately and self-consciously 'Scottish' in one's writing is not to have regained that lost consciousness.

Additional Essays

15

The Scots 'Aeneid' of Gavin Douglas

The medieval Scots poetry of Henryson and Dunbar leads us to Gavin Douglas. But he is no more than they simply a Scottish Chaucerian. He is in a tradition in which the alliterative poetry was still powerful; and though his *Aeneid* is in rhymed couplets—as are Chaucer's *Legend of Good Women* and most of the Canterbury Tales—the movement of its verse is more like that of the alliterative poetry. Chaucer's verse is gently, easily flowing, light, bright, and sparkling. (One cannot dissociate the rhythm from the meaning and whole effect.) The movement of Douglas' verse is characteristically impeded; the heavy, loaded, clogged lines do not flow. This is not artistic incompetence: it is simply another kind of verse, having affinities with the alliterative verse. It can be most expressive when what is being communicated *is* a sense of effort and struggle, strain and stress. It is not at all like Chaucer's verse—and it is not at all like Virgil's.

Douglas' *Aeneid* is also a very different poem from Dryden's. For one thing, it is pre-Miltonic. Dryden's *Aeneid*, in spite of the fact that it is in heroic couplets and not Miltonic blank verse, would not be the kind of thing it is if Dryden had not fallen under the spell of *Paradise Lost*. Dryden had had a great deal of practice in composing heroic plays for the Restoration theatre. But his *Aeneid* is operatic rather than dramatic; it is rhetorical, sonorous, pompous, and full of eloquent speeches— the equivalent (one might argue) of Roman eloquence. Douglas, on the other hand, has a directness of expression that is

Chaucerian and, indeed, medieval. We find the same kind of directness in Dante and Villon. It is not 'Chaucerian' in the sense that it is merely imitated from Chaucer; it is something Douglas shared with Chaucer: a quality of the medieval vernaculars, the speech of medieval people. By asserting that Douglas' *Aeneid* is a better poem than Virgil's, Pound at least drew attention (though with Middle West violence) to the possibility that Douglas' translation might have merits of its own. It was reckless to assert that it is a *better* poem. But it is certainly a *different* poem from Virgil's, a poem in its own right, and it requires to be judged as such. And that is what, I suppose, Pound wanted recognized.

One might perhaps say that Douglas' *Aeneid* and Virgil's are different as Chaucer's *Troilus and Criseyde* is different from Boccaccio's *Il Filostrato*. But Chaucer and Boccaccio were at least contemporaries. Chaucer's England and Boccaccio's Italy were not centuries apart as are Douglas' Scotland and Virgil's Rome. Chaucer, of course, does something more than translate; he rearranges and amplifies, reshapes his material freely; he deliberately and consciously *makes* a new poem in the English language out of his Italian material.

Douglas, on the other hand, is a close translator. His whole endeavour, clearly, was to be faithful to his much respected original. Yet the miracle is that the result again is a new, a different poem. The whole effect could not be more different from that of the poetry of Virgil's *Aeneid*. The differences are radical: the differences between two languages (Douglas' Scots and Virgil's Latin), between two civilizations (medieval Christian and Augustan Roman).

Douglas certainly was not so conscious of the differences between himself and the Roman poet as are modern scholars. It may be said that not to be conscious of those differences means a failure to understand—through inadequate knowledge. But consciousness of differences may itself become a barrier, produce a failure of sympathy which in its turn may prevent a deeper, fuller understanding. Douglas could scarcely avoid being conscious of differences of language, since he was struggling with these throughout his arduous labour of translation. On the other hand, Latin was a language still in written and spoken use in Gavin Douglas' community—that of the medieval Church and the whole body of the clerks throughout medieval Christendom. Douglas was a medieval bishop, a clerk, as well as a Scotsman; to that extent his language was Latin as well as Scots.

But there is no sign that he was much troubled by any sense of a radical difference between his civilization and Virgil's. He had not our historical sense. For him, the poet Virgil was 'a man speaking to men'. Eliminate the nineteenth-century historical sense, and Virgil becomes—what in effect he was for Douglas—a contemporary. The difference Douglas was most conscious of was rather that Virgil was an exalted poet, high in the hierarchy of the world's clerks, an illustrious 'authority', whom Douglas regarded with reverence as being nearly associated with the Fathers of the Church. This is very like Dante's attitude to Virgil. Douglas clearly has a reverence for Virgil such as Chaucer could not have for Boccaccio, and it affects his attitude as a translator.

We modern readers *can* sometimes feel about a Roman poet —about Catullus or Horace or Propertius—quite suddenly that, after all, he is a man just like ourselves. The differences of language, of civilization, the centuries between, suddenly fall away in the moment of communication. There is the sudden sympathy, the flash of understanding. But, in the case of these poets, it often comes at the moment of our recognition of their human weaknesses, when we have *least* reverence for the man who was the poet. The differences between their civilization and ours are also part of what is communicated in their poetry, but at such moments it is no longer the essential part. Douglas reveres his poet, but there *is* at the same time an understanding, a sympathy which is direct, not interfered with by any historical sense. Modern readers, perhaps overburdened by their historical sense, easily become preoccupied with the differences between themselves and the poets of the past, over-emphasize these, and so make communication more difficult; for, unless we can recognize some common human experience, there can be no direct communication.

Since Douglas was innocent of our historical sense, he was spared the need of a conscious effort to make his Virgil modern. For Douglas, Virgil was as modern as himself, that is to say as medieval; Virgil was another medieval poet. Douglas is not a post-Renaissance humanist as are Ben Jonson and, to some extent, Shakespeare in their attitudes to the Classics. The *Aeneid* does not open out a new, a different world to Douglas. Shakespeare's Roman plays do convey the sense of a larger, more spacious, nobler, more splendid world than that of his Elizabethan England. Shakespeare's Rome, with its chimney-pots, is still to some extent Shakespeare's own London; its reality—the realism of its presentation—depends on its relation to Shakespeare's own immediate London experience. But it is at the same time different, London and yet Rome—the Rome of Plutarch, Seneca and the Classics. It has this kind of complex reality; it has something of both cities. Douglas has his immediate Scottish medieval experience, but he lacks Shakespeare's and Ben Jonson's imaginative ability to move outside his own limited experience, to project himself into a world which he recognizes to be different from his own. Douglas' *Aeneid* is thus not 'translation' in the larger sense that something new is brought across from one civilization to another; no new vision is communicated; the mind does not pass through a vista to a new, a different world. Douglas has resisted Virgil's Latin; he is impervious to many of the differences implied in it. His translation is, therefore, not a new poem of the kind that might have produced a revolution in poetry, new ways of thinking and feeling. Ben Jonson's translations and paraphrases from the Latin poets do so; racily English, they are at the same time new in English poetry.[1] They introduce Latin qualities that are to be found present in the poetry of his successors, the Caroline poets, and in Marvell,

[1] This whole subject has recently been treated by Harold Mason in his distinguished book *Humanism and Poetry in the Early Tudor Period* (1959).

and again in new variations in Dryden, Pope and Samuel Johnson's imitations of Horace and Juvenal. But the civilized Roman world presents no challenge to Douglas' medieval Christian world; he simply does not recognize it as different and alien.

Yet Douglas has a strength inseparable from his limitations. His endeavour—with medieval humility—is to submit to the authority of his text, to be faithful, to be accurate. One can see that his extensions and elaborations are often intended simply to be explanatory, to the end that the meaning of his original may be more fully understood. There is an element of pedantry, even of pedagogy, in Douglas as translator. But because Douglas is a poet, a maker, a master of his own language, the result is poetry. Translation, the endeavour to be faithful to his original, brought the whole of himself into play. His method of translating (one can see) was to endeavour as fully as possible to 'realize' the meaning—to imagine each scene, each episode, situation, feeling, as fully as he can, wholly in terms of his own personal and local medieval Scottish experience. In so doing, he finds words in his own spoken Scots language to express that meaning as he has himself conceived and experienced it. His strength, as well as his limitation, is that—never moving outside his own experience—he is yet paradoxically inside the experience he is incorporating in Scots. The result, as I have said, is quite different from Virgil. But the result is poetry.

II

Douglas rises at times to something near great poetry, as Dryden never does in his translation of the *Aeneid*. (Dryden comes nearer great poetry in his translation of Lucretius on death.) There is, in Douglas' *Aeneid*—notably in Book VI— a deeper, a religious and moral seriousness, a medieval gravity. Douglas belongs, after all, to the age of Chaucer and Shakespeare, a larger, more humane and more profound age than that of Dryden.

Hell was as real to the medieval bishop and Scotsman as

Scotland itself. In Douglas' *Aeneid* Hell is in fact Scotland in its wilder aspects, the mountainous and craggy wastes, the gloomy waters, and the wild and lawless inhabitants of these regions, as they might be viewed and feared at the oncoming of night; the medieval poet conceives Hell in these images as a physical—as well as a metaphysical—reality.

Douglas himself describes his Scottish language as harsh and rugged in contrast to Virgil's sonorous and sophisticated Latin, but he could, and does, make full use of its characteristic powers in embodying his Scottish landscape of Hell. There is nothing here in his actual translation—whatever he has said in his prologue to his translation—like Tennyson's ambition to make English sound as much like Italian as possible. Dryden, in his *Aeneid*, in this respect approximates more to the Virgilian Latin sonority and mellifluousness. The vigour of Dryden's language in his satires is excluded from his translation of Virgil.

Douglas' version of the descent of Aeneas to the underworld does not become explicitly moral allegory. But it is inevitably affected by the habit of moral allegory implanted in the medieval religious imagination, particularly the vision of earthly life as a journey through uncharted waste regions, treacherous, perilous both to body and soul.

Here is Douglas' 'Invocation desiring pardon or he begin to schaw the secretis of hell':

> O ye goddis, in quhais power and mycht
> The sawlis bene, and ye derne[1] skuggis[2] dirk,
> Confusit Chaos, quhairof all thing bene wirk,
> Scaldand hellis flude, Flagiton, but[3] lycht,
> Placis of silence and perpetuall nycht!
> Mot it be leifull to me for to tell
> Thai thingis quhilkis I haif hard sayde of hell,
> And, by your mychtis, that I may furth schaw
> Seir[4] thingis drinchit in the erd full law,
> And deip involvit in mirknes and in mist.

There is no mistaking its deep seriousness. It has the note of personal prayer, intimate, sincere, the note of humility in the

[1] secret.   [2] shadows.   [3] without.   [4] various.

presence of what is beyond common experience. Douglas is awed by the near presence of the experience on the threshold of which he stands, and he is fully possessed by that experience when it comes upon him. Christian religious feeling (as in Dante) has deepened, or at least altered, the seriousness of Virgil. 'Placis of silence and perpetuall nycht' renders 'loca nocti tacentia late'. 'Perpetuall'—taken up later by 'quhair ever is nycht and never lycht dois repair'—introduces an emphasis that is not in the Virgil. It is there again in the surprisingly Dantesque passage in the youthful Shakespearean poetry of *Richard III*.

> I past, methought, the melancholy flood,
> With that grim ferryman which poets write of,
> Unto the kingdom of perpetual night.

The foggy, murky northern nights (Lady Macbeth's 'Hell is murky') are inseparable from the way Douglas senses Hell.

> . . . And deip involvit in mirknes and in mist.[1]
> Thai walkand furth, sa dirk uneth[2] thai wist
> Quhiddir thai went, amyd dym schaddowis thair,
> Quhair ever is nycht and never lycht dois repair,
> Throwout the waist dongeon of Pluto king,
> Thai voyde boundis and that gousty ring;
> Siclyke as quha wald throw thik woddis wend
> In obscure lycht, quhair mone may nocht be kend,
> As Jupiter, the king etherial,
> With erdis scug[3] hydis the hevynis all,
> And the myrk nycht, with hir visage gray,
> From every thing hes reft the hew away.

The atmosphere in Douglas is thicker, denser than in Virgil. (As in *Macbeth* the smothering darkness: 'the blanket of the dark'—'come, thick night'—'hover through the fog and filthy air'.) 'Gousty' is more atmospheric, more Gothic than Virgil's 'inania'. The image of night stealing away the colours of things is in Chaucer also (*Troilus and Criseyde*, Book II, 908–9):

> And white thynges wexen dymme and donne
> For lak of lyght.

[1] 'mist' is not in Virgil.   [2] scarcely.   [3] shadow.

But anything corresponding to 'mirk' or to the force and violence of 'reft' is more rare in Chaucer.[1] 'Visage gray' is not in Virgil, but it is Chaucerian (and, indeed, Dantean). Night inevitably becomes for the medieval poet a distinct, visualized person.

The image helps to make the transition to the passage of personifications who *are* already there in Virgil, as presences thronging round the threshold of the underworld. Here Douglas is presented with the task of rendering experience with which, as a medieval poet, he is completely at home, images with which the medieval imagination constantly consorted.

> Befoir the port and first jawis of hell,
> Lamentatioun and wraikfull[2] Thochtis fell
> Thair lugeing had; and thairat dwellis eik
> Pail Maladeis, that causis folk be seik;
> The feirfull Dreid, and als unweildy Age,
> The felloun Hungir with hir undantit rage:
> Thair wes also the laithlie Indigence,
> Terrible of port, and schamefull hir presence;
> The grislie Deid, that mony ane hes slane,
> The hard Laubour and disseisfull Pane,
> The slottry[3] Sleip, Deidis cusing[4] of kynd,
> Inordinat Blythnis of perversit mynd;
> And in the yet,[5] forganis thaim, did stand
> The mortale Battele with his deidlie brand,
> The irn chalmeris[6] of hellis Fureis fell,
> Witles Discord, that woundring[7] maist crewell,
> Wymplit and buskit in a bludy bend,
> With snakis hung at every hairis end.

The personifications become fully embodied presences in Douglas' translation,[8] assuming almost the same degree of vividness

[1] That is what Hopkins also, in *Spelt from Sibyl's Leaves*, felt was so terrible about the oncoming of night; it drains away the 'dapple' of things; it takes away their shapes and colours and identities.

[2] revengeful. [3] drowsy. [4] cousin. [5] gate.
[6] chambers. [7] monster.

[8] e.g. the following italicized phrases are among those not in Virgil: Pail Maladeis, *that causis folk be seik* . . . the *grislie* Deid, *that mony ane hes slane.*

as in the passage on the Temple of Mars in Chaucer's *Knight's Tale*.

By comparison with Douglas, Dryden is not serious enough. He frequently stiffens his rhetoric by his characteristic formal balance and neatness, his formal precision; but it is here often an appearance of precision only, neat verbal formulation empty of experience and suggestion.

> Forms without bodies and impassive air.

Language is here moving towards abstraction and generalization; as definition of experience it is not so precise as it seems or sounds.

In his renderings of the descriptions, earlier in the sixth book, of the forests in which is the golden bough, Dryden works up a vague Miltonic impressiveness, too literary, too poetical, heavily adjectival with his 'deep forests and impenetrable night'—'infernal bounds'—'sable waves'—'trembling shades' —'gloomy night'—

> the branch
> Whose glittering shadow gilds the sacred ground.

Douglas finds his way through Virgil by keeping close to his own immediate experience (see *his* description of the golden bough).

The entrance to the otherworld becomes in Douglas' Scots a cave he might have come across among his Scottish mountains, a cave associated with hell by local belief.

> Thar stud a dirk and profound cave fast by,
> Ane hiddouis hole, deip gapand and grisly,
> All full of craggis and of thir scherp flint stanis,
> Quhilk wes weill dekkit and closit for the nanis
> With a foull laik, als blak as ony craw,
> And skuggis dym of a full dern wod schaw,
> Abufe the quhilk na foull may fle but[1] skaith.

Hell is associated by Douglas, as by Shakespeare in *Macbeth*, with 'black things of night' and the crow that 'makes wing to the rooky wood'. 'Scherp flint stanis' and 'blak as ony craw' are not in Virgil.

[1] without.

In the Charon episode Douglas (as Dante does in Canto III of the *Inferno*) *sees* the place and the ferryman and the crowd on the bank all over again. What he loses in sonority he gains in dramatizing energy through, and by means of, his Scots. The vigour of his Scots is brought into play and used not simply for its sound-values (though he does make use of sound-effects in reproducing the noises made by the rivers of Hell) but to embody the experience.

> Fra thine strekis[1] the way profound anon
> Deip onto hellis flude of Acheron;
> With holl bisme,[2] and hiduus swelth unrude,
> Drumlie of mud, and scaldand as it wer wod,[3]
> Popland[4] and bullerand[5] furth on athir hand
> Onto Cochitus all his slik[6] and sand.
> Thir riveris and thir watteris kepit war
> By ane Charon, a grislie ferriar,
> Terrible of schap, and sluggert of array:
> Apon his chin feill cannos[7] haris gray,
> Lyart[8] feltat[9] tatis;[10] with birnand ene reid,
> Like tua fire blesis fixit in his heid . . .
> This ald hasard[11] careis our[12] fludis hoit
> Spretis and figuris in his irn hewit boit,
> Allthocht he eildit was, or step[13] in age,
> Als fery[14] and als swippir[15] as a page;
> For in a god the age is fresche and grene . . .
> Thiddir to the bray swarmit all the rout
> Of deid gaistis, and stud the bank about;
> Baith matrouns, and thair husbandis, all yferis,[16]
> Ryall princis, and nobill chevaleris,
> Small childrin, and young damicellis unwed,
> And fair springaldis[17] laitlie deid in bed,
> In fader and in moderis presens laid on beir.
> Als gret number thiddir thikkit in feir;
> As in the first frost eftir hervist tyde,
> Levis of treis in the wod doith slyde;
> Or birdis flokkis our the fludis gray,

[1] stretches. [2] abyss. [3] mad. [4] bubbling.
[5] rushing noise. [6] mud, slime. [7] hoary. [8] gray.
[9] matted. [10] uncombed locks. [11] dotard.
[12] over. [13] advanced. [14] brisk. [15] nimble.
[16] together. [17] striplings.

> Onto the land seikand the nerrest way,
> Quhom the cald sesoun cachis our the sea,
> Into sum benar[1] realm and warm countre . . .

The experience is partly of a place—its quality, its atmosphere —and of a character, 'ane Charon, a grislie ferriar' who belongs there, an embodiment of the spirit of the place. There is something oddly familiar about that old ferryman and his 'irn hewit boit', and about the place; at the same time something unfamiliar, ghostly, uncanny. A wayfarer might have met, among the mountain wastes, such an old man—a native of the place—and felt that he is more, or other, than he seems. (Wordsworth recovers such a feeling about his old men unexpectedly met with among the desolate moors.) He is reminiscent of the medieval allegorical Age (Elde) associated with Death. He is also a demonic power, with his 'birnand ene reid'. The phrase renders Virgil's 'stant lumina flamma'. In Virgil, Charon is a god; in Dante, he is explicitly a demon 'Charon dimonio' (Charon the demon with eyes of glowing coal . . . the steersman on the livid marsh who round his eyes had wheels of fire). In Douglas, he is all these things: a ferryman one might come across in a waste region, whose services one might require to ferry one across a gloomy water at nightfall; Age associated with Death; a demon on the borderland of Hell.

The crowd of dead people on the shore are Douglas' medieval contemporaries and, at the same time, ghostly like the London crowd that seemed to Wordsworth like a second-sight procession, or the crowd that flowed over London Bridge, so many

> I had not thought death had undone so many.

The comparisons of that crowd on the shore to falling leaves and migrating birds that introduce the late-autumn note in the poetry are, in Douglas, close both to Virgil and to observed fact.

The passage in which Charon takes Aeneas aboard and the living warrior weighs down the leaky boat completes the experience of the place in Douglas' version.

[1] more pleasant, agreeable.

175

His watry hewit boit, haw[1] lyke the se,
Toward thaim turnis and addressis he,
And gan approche onto the bra in haist:
Syne uther saulis expellit hes and chaist
Furth of his bait, quhilk sat endlang the wail:[2]
He strekit[3] sone his airis, and graithis[4] his sail,
And thairwithall the big wechty Enee
Within his weschall boddum rasavis he.
Under the paysand[5] and the hevy charge[6]
Gan grane[7] or geig[8] ful fast the jonit[9] barge,
Sa full of riftis, and with lekkis perbraik,[10]
Scho suppit huge wattir of the laik.
Bot, at the last, attour the flude yit than
Salflie scho brocht baith prophetes and man,
And furth thaim sett amyd the foul glar,
Amang the fauch rispis[11] harsk[12] and star.[13]

Dryden's version of the same episode is relatively effective in *its* context. Perhaps he had watched a ship loaded with merchandise on the Thames. Dryden has a post-Hobbesian feeling for mass, weight, matter, lumpishness; but the experience remains an ordinary, everyday transaction.

Neither Dryden nor Douglas, indeed, have a feeling for the magic a post-romantic reader might feel in Virgil. This matter-of-factness can, however, become a positive strength in Douglas. Whenever, for example, he has to do with boats and navigation, the sea and the weather, he is unmistakably writing from first-hand knowledge; and he has a feeling for water and the sea as have his predecessors, the Northern alliterative poets. But both Douglas and Dryden miss the effect of, for example,

Tendebantque manus ripae ulterioris amore

(or, in Book I,

Sunt lacrimae rerum et mentem mortalia tangunt).

They could not have *heard* the Latin, at least not in the way

[1] pale, wan.   [2] gunwale.   [3] extends.   [4] prepares.
[5] weighty.   [6] burden.   [7] groan.   [8] creak.
[9] joined.   [10] broken.   [11] reeds.   [12] rough.
[13] stiff.

that Tennyson taught a generation to listen. The Romantics
do seem to have made subsequent readers conscious of effects
and qualities in Virgil which earlier translators and readers
missed.

Douglas, however, reveals a deeper humanity than Dryden's
Aeneid ever does, a human intimacy and Christian gentleness
that again remind one of Chaucer.

> Young babbeis saulis weping sor thai hard;
> Quham the hasty and blak duleful day
> Sowkand thar moderis pap had reft away,
> From the sweit lyf twynnit[1] untymusly.

This corresponds to the Virgilian tenderness and sadness, and
sense of the 'tears in things'. 'Voices . . . the souls of infants
weeping . . . on the very threshold of sweet life . . . torn from
the breast, the black day swept away . . .'

> Voces . . . infantumque animae flentes, in limine primo
> quos dulcis vitae exsortis et ab ubere raptos
> abstulit atra dies . . .

By comparison, Dryden is rhetorical and frigid.

> Before the gates, the cries of babes new-born
> Whom Fate had from their tender mothers torn
> Assault his ears . . .

The meeting of Aeneas with Dido among the shades and
Dido's disdainful withdrawal is, in Virgil's *Aeneid*, expressive
of the most civilized, delicate feeling, the most sensitive tact.
Douglas' rendering disappoints, not only judged by our post-
Romantic sensibility but by any objective comparison a
modern reader is capable of making with Virgil. (The final
meeting of Troilus and Cresseid at the end of Henryson's
Testament, the moment of half-recognition when yet 'not ane
ane uther knew', is more poignant.) Yet here again Douglas
is a more profound poet than Dryden. For Dryden, Dido's
social status and public demeanour are all-important; for
Douglas, she is a woman, the tragedy more simply a human
tragedy. 'O fey Dido' means much more than 'unhappy queen'

[1] parted.

in Dryden's context. The episode offers Dryden once more an opportunity for the grand manner, the imperious gesture, the majestic pose. The deeper humanity is lost in the social or public attitude. Dryden's version of Aeneas' speech, too, is a fine speech, but it carries less conviction as an expression of the feeling of a man compelled to separate in obedience to the powerful gods than does Douglas' version.

III

The presentation of a human relationship is perhaps the severest test of any poet, as of any dramatist or novelist; the Dido and Aeneas story is therefore perhaps Douglas' severest test as translator and as a poet. Douglas renders the story as one who knows the power of passion—as do Chaucer and Henryson before him—and at the same time views it as a medieval Christian moralist, for whom human love must always be subordinate to obedience to the divine will. This may not be exactly what Virgil meant by *pietas*, by obeying the decrees of the gods, by submitting to destiny, but it is the medieval Christian equivalent or development from it. He understands *Amor* as a power hard to control, a consuming fire—as in Virgil and as in Dante ('the ancient flame') and Petrarch (whether or not Douglas read the Italian poets). He equally well understands the obedience of *pius Aeneas* to the will of the gods, the destiny imposed on him, and that Dido must be sacrificed—a thing more hard for us to accept: the sacrifice of a human individual and human feelings to some (perhaps illusory) conception of duty or destiny. Douglas understands, as a medieval Christian. Do we, perhaps, coming after the Romantics, romanticize the Dido and Aeneas story? There is unmistakably, as I have said, a fineness of feeling, a tact, a civilized quality in Virgil's rendering. Virgil is more sensitive to subtle shades of experience; he is less simple than Douglas. Dryden, for whom women are 'the fair sex', is by comparison coarse, even vulgar, as the Restoration was in its attitude to love. Romantic taste has perhaps enabled us to feel qualities that are actually there in Virgil and that Douglas missed—though Douglas was in the tradition of courtly love—qualities which Dryden certainly missed. We can be conscious of our debt to the Romantics, without falling into what is perhaps their error of regarding romantic love as the supreme or absolute value. Douglas renders the story of passion with simple dignified humanity, yet with a firm, even harsh, recognition that it is contrary to the divine will and purpose.

Dryden's rendering of the Dido and Aeneas story is in resonance with his *All for Love* and with Purcell's opera *Dido and Aeneas*. We meet again the qualities of *All for Love*, rhetorical, grandiose, pompous, sonorous, theatrical, operatic. We are never allowed to forget that this is passion on the grand scale, in the heroic manner, between a queen and a hero of the Ancient World. Dido's status as a queen is undermined, and she suffers agonies of shame. Aeneas has his duty as a hero, a prince. The theme is essentially secularized.

When Virgil and, after him, Dante and Douglas speak of love as fire, they do so with an awed recognition of the power and reality of passionate love.

> adgnosco veteris vestigia flammae.

Dante uses the same phrase, knowing fully what it means. So also Douglas: 'the ald fyre . . . the blynd fyre . . .'

> The brym[1] fury glidis throw out hir banis
> . . . . the subtell quent[2] fyre
> Waistis and consumis merch,[3] banis, and lyre.[4]

Dryden has

> Too like the sparkles of my former flame . . .
> But will you fight against a pleasing flame? . . .
> Saw Dido fettered in the chains of love.

'Pleasing flame' and 'fettered in the chains of love' belong to the worn-out phraseology of love in Dryden's Restoration time.

[1] fierce.   [2] quaint, curious.   [3] marrow.   [4] flesh.

179

We sometimes say that the Restoration degraded love by recognizing only its physical aspect. Rather, Dryden and his contemporaries—if we compare them with Donne and the Metaphysicals—had no real respect for the body and had as little sense of its reality as they had of the reality of the soul. But Douglas reaches through the words to the core of the passionate experience itself, as something in Dido's body, corporeal, physiological, yet right in the centre of her being and absorbing the whole of herself. When it is thwarted as a creative energy (associated with the building of Carthage and founding a city and kingdom) it becomes destructive, as the fire which ultimately consumes her—the fire of her funeral pyre. Douglas' translating is a constant endeavour to enter fully into the experience behind Virgil's words.

How much of Douglas' insight into the human heart did he gain directly from Chaucer, the Chaucer of *Troilus and Criseyde*? There are passages in his version of Virgil's Book IV which express what can only be called a Chaucerian knowledge of human nature and behaviour. They are even reminiscent of particular passages and phrases in Chaucer; yet they cannot be dismissed as mere imitations of the master. The Chaucer who created Criseyde has aided Douglas to attain a fuller insight of his own into Virgil.

> Begyn scho wald to tell furth hir intent,
> And in the myd word stop, and hald hir still:
> And quhen the evin coyme, it wes hir will
> To seik wayis hym to feist, as sche did air;[1]
> And, half myndles, agane sche langis sair
> For tyll inquyre and heir the sege of Troy.

('Half myndles' recalls Dorigen in *The Franklin's Tale*:

> And she answerede half as she were mad.)

Dido, unable to forget the impression Aeneas has made on her, unable to sleep, his image present even when he is absent, is extraordinarily like Criseyde.

[1] before.

> And the declyning of the sternis brycht
> To sleip and rest perswadis every wycht,
> Within her chalmer allane scho langis sair,
> And thocht all waist for lak of hir lufair.
> Amyd ane woid bed scho hir laid adoun,
> And of him absent thinkis scho heris the soun;
> His voce scho heris, and him behaldis sche,
> Thocht he, God wait, fer from her presence be.

The first appearance of Dido (Book I) has much of the quality
of Criseyde's first appearance to Troilus in the temple. Douglas, like Chaucer, has the May festival very much in mind, and
has captured or recaptured something of Chaucer's freshness
and humanity, the note of spring and youthful delight.

> The quene Dido, excellent in bewtie,
> To temple cummis with ane fair menie[1]
> Of lustie yonkeris walking hir about.
> Lyik to the goddes Diane with hir rout,
> Endlang the fluide of Eurot on the bra,
> Or under the toppis of hir hill Cynthea,
> Ledland ring dancis . . .

Douglas finds his way back through the May rites of his contemporary medieval world to the pagan rites of Virgil's Italy,
or rather he is conscious of no essential difference in this
respect between Virgil's world and his own. So also Douglas'
Aeneas, as he first appears to Dido, is Youth and steps out of
the world of the *Romance of the Rose* and of Chaucer.

> . . . full of fresch bewte,
> Lyk till ane yonkeir with two lauchand ene.

(The 'twa lauchand ene' are not in Virgil.) The passages about
the worship of Apollo in Book IV and about the Elysian fields
in Book VI are similar.

> As for to dansing, and to leid the ring,
> To sing ballattis and go in karaling.

This, for Douglas, is being modern, that is to say medieval—
Virgil understood through contemporary poetry and life.

[1] company.

181

In his rendering of the banquet scene that follows in Book I, the serious, moral Douglas brings out the element of deceitfulness in the situation in which Dido and Aeneas quickly become involved by the power of love—'fraudfull luif' with its 'fals subtilite'—Cupid being present in the innocent-seeming form of Ascanius.

> The schyning vissage of the god Cupyte,
> And his dissemelit slekit[1] wordis quhyte . . .
> . . . fenyeand luif full fals . . .
> Full slelie than he blent[2] apon the quene.

And there is the Chaucerian recognition of Dido's human weakness:

> . . . the fey unsely Dido,
> For the mischeif to cum predestinate,
> Mycht not refrene nor satisfy hir consaite.

Dryden renders the banquet scene again in the spirit of *All for Love* (and *Alexander's Feast*), the spirit in which he read or misread *Antony and Cleopatra*. The emphasis of his descriptive rhetoric is on pomp and splendour, luxury and indulgence. The Renaissance taste for splendour and luxury goes on through the periods of baroque and rococo—'wandering foliage and rich flowers entwined'—coarsening in the Restoration. In the treatment of passionate love the phrasing betrays the superficiality and vulgarity of the Restoration.

> . . . the sweet deceit . . .
> Works in the pliant bosom of the fair . . .
> . . . She took him to her arms
> With greedy pleasure and devoured his charms.
> . . . embraced the bowl
> With pleasure swilled the gold nor ceased to draw
> Till he the bottom of the brimmer saw.

Dryden associates the court of Dido with oriental luxury and debauch. He is indulgent and gross, and shows up badly by comparison with the disapproving moral seriousness and deeper insight of Douglas.

[1] sleek, smooth.   [2] glanced.

For the great hunting episode in Book IV we have the good luck to have Chaucer's version in *The Legend of Good Women* with which we may compare the versions of Douglas and Dryden. There is little doubt that in translating this episode Douglas was unable to keep Chaucer's version out of his mind, even if he had wanted to do so. The scene has its full value as splendid spectacle, presented by Douglas with a Chaucerian vividness to ear and eye. But, in addition, Douglas conveys something more essentially Chaucerian still—perhaps captures it directly from Chaucer's version—not simply the pageantry, the outward spectacle, but the glow of life and the note of spring, the fresh vitality, the eagerness, the delighted sense of morning and youth and adventure.

> Furth of the see, with this, the dawing springis . . .
> Joly and glaid the fresche Ascanius ying . . .
> Als fresch, als lusty did Eneas ryde.

The nearest thing to it, outside Chaucer himself, is in the early plays of Shakespeare.

> Was that the king that spurred his horse so hard
> Against the steep uprising of the hill . . .
> > (*Love's Labour's Lost.*)

> Night's candles are burnt out and jocund day
> Stands tiptoe on the misty mountain tops.
> > (*Romeo and Juliet.*)

Dryden's

> The young Ascanius with a sprightly grace

is frigid by comparison; the freshness has evaporated. Douglas is uninflated and direct, in this respect again closer to Chaucer. For Dryden's 'the slow Queen', which suggests a ceremonial slowness, a queenly state, Douglas has the explanatory and human 'that lang in chalmer dwellis'. For Dryden's 'lofty courser', conscious of its 'majestic' rider, we have in Douglas 'hir fers steid stude stamping', which expresses something more like Chaucer's feeling for the living creature, spirited, nervous, impatient, held in. In Douglas, Aeneas is simply a

183

man rather than a personage, and therefore the comparison of him with the god Apollo has a sudden genuinely enhancing, glorifying effect; for a moment he is seen as Dido sees him, with the eyes of love.

The pagan rites and feasts in worship of Apollo easily become for Douglas, as for Chaucer, the May rites and dances which belong both to the popular and to the courtly life of their own times.

> Renewand ringis and dancis, mony a rowt . . .
> Schowtand on ther gise[1] with clamour and vocis hie . . .
> With a soft garland of lawrere sweit smelling.

Apollo, in Dryden, is merely the secularized great personage who presides over the revels, gives commands, like Louis XIV. The festival is

> The merry madness of the sacred show.

It is looked upon from outside, as the fine gentlemen of Restoration London or the Court of Charles II might look upon a rustic merry-making. It is merely a 'show'—the essential feeling of 'sacred' is lost—and it is regarded as behaviour that is not rational but probably a drunken debauch. We are left to admire Dryden's stylistic sophistication, the balanced phrases, the formal neatness which, in the description, help to maintain the detachment from the contemplated 'sacred show'. For Douglas'

> Als fresch, als lusty did Eneas ryde;
> With als gret bewtie in his lordlie face

Dryden has

> . . . not less the prince is seen
> In manly presence or in lofty mien.

Aeneas is the prince, the royal personage; his attitude, his presence, his mien are what is important. In addition, there is the kind of 'manliness' that Dryden admired, the masculine vigour, the virility (which he celebrates so genially and com-

[1] custom.

plaisantly in Charles II in the opening of *Absalom and Achitophel*).

The hunt itself is clearly one of the things that Douglas could feel he had in common with Virgil. As a member of one of the great families of Scotland, belonging to a time and country in which hunting was still a necessary as well as an aristocratic activity, Douglas could feel, in translating Virgil, that he was entering into a description of something he knew about. The hunt is a splendid royal occasion but at the same time a practical, purposeful expedition in a wild country.

> With ralis and with nettis strang and wyde,
> And hunting speris stif with hedis braid.

Douglas conveys the actuality of the hunt as a practical activity, a strenuous exertion in Scottish country with Scottish weather. His

> The hepe of dust upstouring at thair taill

is more specific and vivid than Dryden's 'dusty plain'. Douglas' broken rhythms convey the sense of effortful action, obstructed erratic movement.

> Now makkis his renk[1] yondir, and now this way,
> Now prekis furth by thir, and now by thaim.

The famous storm that causes Dido and Aeneas to seek refuge in a cave is in Douglas a commotion of the elements as it might be actually experienced among the Scottish mountains. He has the resources of language for this kind of presentation, and the skill which his predecessors, the Northern alliterative poets, had long practised.

> . . . the hevinnis all about
> With fellon noyis gan to rummyll and rowt.
> A bub of weddir followit in the taill,
> Thik schour of rane myddillit full of haill.

Douglas here enlarges on Virgil's description with details from his own Scottish experience of thunderstorms and floods.

> Thai seik to haldis, housis, hirnis[2] and beildis.[3]

---

[1] course.   [2] corners.   [3] shelters.

This line gives in more detail than the original Virgil the diversity of places to which the members of the splendid cavalcade, poor mortals after all, scatter to seek shelter. Dryden has 'homely cots or mountain's hollow sides'. 'Homely cots' belongs with the pastoral or Horatian landscape of minor seventeenth- to eighteenth-century poetry; it belongs with

> . . . the mountain goats; they bound
> From rock to rock

(in a preceding passage in Dryden's *Aeneid*).

In Dryden the episode of the hunt, the storm and the cave is a Court idyll, a Court intrigue in a pastoral or sylvan setting, treated in the grand manner because Dido and Aeneas are royal personages. The departure for the hunt is a ceremonial occasion, as at the Court of Versailles; and the martial note is not absent—to emphasize the heroic aspect.

> The brawny guards in martial order stand.

The style is elevated to correspond to the seventeenth-century idea of the Homeric epic and of Court state and ceremony in an absolute monarchy.

> Her lofty courser, in the court below,
> Who his majestic rider seems to know,
> Proud of his purple trappings, paws the ground.

Throughout his *Aeneid* Dryden thus sacrifices the virtues of his own best poetry for a grandiose impressiveness. Douglas, following Chaucer, can conclude the whole episode with the simple and poignant recognition of the alternating joy and sorrow of human lives in which Dido and Aeneas have their share.

> This was the foremast day of hir glaidnes,
> And first morow of hir wofull distres.

Chaucer's version is undoubtedly the finest, the most delicate and subtle of the three. It not only conveys most fully the value of the scene as splendid spectacle, chivalric pageantry it communicates the glow of life and movement, the sense of youth ('o yonge fresshe folkes'), and all with an ease not simply of manner but of spirit. The poetry is both urbane and gently human.

> And she is fair as is the brighte morwe
> That heleth seke folk of nightes sorwe.

The gentleness, the compassion seems to add even to Virgil a new dimension—perhaps of Christian feeling—a fuller humanity. Chaucer is able to take 'a central, a truly human point of view'.

> . . . this was the firste morwe
> Of hir gladnesse, and ginning of hir sorwe.

Assuming that Chaucer had the same text before him, this is a mistranslation of

> ille dies primus leti primusque malorum
> causa fuit,

a mistranslation apparently followed by Douglas. But it might be called a felicitous mistranslation in that the effect is more Chaucerian than would be the correct translation. The note of glad acceptance of life is characteristic of Chaucer; but so is also the clear recognition of human frailties and the vicissitudes of the earthly condition. Here, as so often in Chaucer, we have a sense of the complexity of life as being at one and the same moment—it is the basic irony—comedy and tragedy. Nothing is over-emphasized; everything is seen in proportion to everything else. The occasional humour is delicately controlling and controlled, objectifying the subject. The sudden storm breaks in—like 'the smoky rain' in *Troilus and Criseyde* —and plays its part in what, for Chaucer, is a profoundly human drama. Virgil communicates in this episode an effect of a sudden conjunction of circumstances, a fateful swift succession of events. He has more intensity, a more tragic sense of fate, but not perhaps the same large and full sense of complex life.

The ghosts and apparitions, dreams and nightmares in the story of Dido have unusual reality in Douglas' version. They are felt to be not merely images in the mind but intruders upon one's life. For Douglas (as for Shakespeare), whatever his personal beliefs, it was in some ways to his advantage as a poet that he and his audience belonged to an age and country in which there were still powerful popular superstitions. One gets the impression that Chaucer himself was singularly free from these things though he can, and occasionally does, vividly present a ghostly presence at the bedside. Douglas' version (Book I) of the ghostly image of Dido's dead husband who appears to her in sleep has this Chaucerian vividness.

> Bot of hir husband bigravit[1] the image
> To hir aperis in sleip, with paill visage . . .
> He schew the knyfe out throw his breist threst.[2]

When, as in Donne's *Apparition*, Dido threatens to revenge herself on Aeneas by haunting him after her death as an angry menacing ghost (Book IV) the medieval terror of death and of Hell as grim realities gives Douglas' Scots version its particular force.

> With fyre infernale, in thine absence also,
> I sall the follow; and, fra the cald deid
> Reif fro my membris this saull, in every steid
> My gost sal be present the to aggrise.[3]

Douglas conveys the ferocity and violence of the offended and outraged Dido, conceived as a half-savage woman (like Medea), a barbarian queen after all, not a civilized Roman or Trojan. Yet death changes and dignifies her, as it seems, if we are to

[1] buried.

[2] Cf. Hector's ghost in Book II.

> His fax* and berd was fadit quhar he stuide,
> And all his hair was glitnit full of bluide.
> > * hair.

Cf. the vanishing of Anchises' ghost in Book V with that of the ghost in *Hamlet*.

> The donk nycht is allmaist rollit away,
> And the fers Orient will that I withdraw;
> I feill the ayndingt of his horsis blaw.
> > Thus has he said; and with that word, but mair,
> Vanist away, as the reik in the air.
> > > † breathing.

[3] terrify.

judge by the episode among the shades (Book VI) when she turns away disdainfully and with dignity, and when we feel that it is Aeneas who is made to look small.

IV

There must still have been a considerable martial element in the late medieval Scottish scene corresponding, for Douglas, to the martial world of the *Aeneid*. There are certainly other correspondences between Virgil's Italy—a mountainous land, after all, with mountain torrents and long sea coasts—and Douglas' Scotland. But to do justice to Douglas we have in the end to set aside Virgil's poem and consider Douglas' *Aeneid* as a Scottish poem. There are things that Douglas can do in his Scots language that are not done better anywhere else. He is particularly at home as a poet of wild landscape, seascape and weather. His versions of the two similes of a river in flood in Book II, for example, are in the fullest sense Scottish poetry made out of Douglas' own experience of 'burns in spate'.

(1) Or quhen the burne on spait hurlis doun the bank,
Othir[1] throw a water brek, or spait of fluide,
Ryvand up reid erd as it war wouide,
Downe dingand cornys, all the plewch labour at anis,
And drivis on swiftlie stoikis,[2] treis and stanis . . .

(2) Nocht sa fersly the fomy rivair or flude
Brekkis our the bankis, on spait quhen it is woude,
And, with his bruscheand faird[3] of watter broun,
The dikis and the schoiris bettis doun,
Ourspredand croftis and flattis with his spait,
Our all the feildis that thai may row ane bait,
Quhill howsis and the flokkis flittis away,
The corne graingis, and standard stakkis off hay . . .[4]

[1] either.   [2] stocks.   [3] force.
[4] Cf. Prologue to Book 7:

Branchis brattlyng, and blayknit* schew the brays,
With hyrstis† harsk of waggand wyndilstrays;‡

* bleached.   † bare hill-sides (?).   ‡ dogs-tail grass.

There are, for instance, no details in Virgil corresponding to 'reid erd' and 'stoikis, treis and stanis' in the first description nor to 'that thai may row ane bait', 'watter broun' and 'corne graingis, and standard stakkis off hay' in the second. The fullness of detail comes from what Douglas has himself witnessed.

The river and the sea, especially floods and storms, are subjects peculiarly Douglas' own. The sole reason Pound offered for his assertion that Douglas' *Aeneid* was a better poem than Virgil's was that Douglas 'had heard the sea'. Certainly Douglas has the sea, his own Northern sea, in his blood. Wherever his poetry has to do with the sea and ships it expresses an intimacy of knowledge that, as a poet, the Bishop has in common with the Northern European alliterative poets, and which he shared with his Scottish seafaring and fishing countrymen and all the Northern seafaring peoples; the sea in his poetry is as his people had learnt to know it in harsh experience. Douglas' Scots language itself is saturated with this traditional knowledge; and (as already remarked) his language, in common with the Teutonic languages, has resources which could be used by Douglas to express, with particular force, the stress and strain of contention with storms at sea.

> Dyrknes as nycht besett the seis abowt;
> The firmament gane rummeling rair and rowt,
> The skyis oft lychtnit with fyry lewyne,[1]
> And schortlie baitht air, sea, and hewyne,
> And every thing mannasit the men to de,
> Schawand the deith present tofor thair ee . . .
> Ane blusterand bub,[2] out fra the northt braying,
>
> The dew droppis congelyt on stibyll and rynd,
> And scharp hailstanis, mortfundit* of kynd,
> Hoppand on the thak and on the causay by.

* cold as death.

[1] lightning.   [2] blast.

Gane our the foirschip[1] in the bak sail dyng,
And to the sternys up the fluide can cast;
The ayris, hachis, and the takillis brast,
The schippis stewyn[2] frawart hir went can writhe,
And turnit hir braid syide to the wallis[3] swithe.[4]
Heich as ane hill the jaw of watter brak,
And in ane heip come on thame with ane swak.
Sum hesit[5] hoverand on the wallis hycht,
And sum the sownchand see so law gart lycht,
Thame semit the erd oppinnit amyd the flude;
The stowr up bullerit[6] sand as it war wuid.

(Book 1.)

This poetry of the sea ranges from practical nautical knowledge—knowledge of sea, sky and weather specifically as these
affect the craft of seamanship—to moments of vision in which
Death becomes an immediate presence, ubiquitous, devouring,
associated in the medieval imagination of the poet with the
horrors of Hell and Damnation. The description of a storm at
sea in Donne's verse letter to Mr. Christopher Brooke expresses the same kind of imaginative vision even more power-
fully, if more idiosyncratically. Douglas' version of Scylla and
Charybdis in Book III are of this imaginative order, expressive
of sea commotions and convulsions washing the stars and
reaching down to Hell.

The large fludis suppis thrise in ane swelth,[7]
And uther quhilis spowtis in the air agane,
Drivand the stour[8] to the sternis, as it war rane.
Bot Scilla lurkand in derne hiddillis[9] lyis
Within hir cave, spreidand hir mouth feil syis[10]
To souk the schippis amang the rolkis unsure . . .
The swelland swirl uphesit us to hevin;
Syne wald the wall swak us doun full evin,
As it apperit, undir the see till hell.

Book V, which like Virgil's original in this part of his poem,
The Odyssy, is especially full of the sea, offers Douglas his
maximum opportunities.

[1] prow.   [2] prow.   [3] waves.   [4] soon.
[5] were lifted up.   [6] churned.   [7] whirlpool.   [8] spray.
          [9] hiding places.   [10] times.

191

> The formy stour of seis rais thair and heir,
> Throw fers bak drauchtis of feil gardeis squair.
> Thai seuch[1] the fludis, that, souchand quhair thai fair,
> In sondir slydis; ourweltit[2] eik with ayris,
> Fra thair foirstammys[3] the buller[4] brayis and raris.

The descriptions of sea-voyaging in the Northern English fourteenth-century alliterative poem *The Destruction of Troy* are, perhaps, the nearest thing to Douglas. But Eliot's *Dry Salvages* (and Pound's *Seafarer*) should help the modern reader to an appreciation of Douglas' sea and river poetry. Douglas' version of the rock exposed in calm weather, washed over by the sea in storms, recalls the same image in *Dry Salvages*.

The characteristics of this poetry of the sea are, in the final analysis, those of Douglas' Scots language. The same characteristics may be apprehended again in Douglas' versions of the simile of the felling of an oak in Book II and of an oak resisting the wind in Book IV. In both instances the poetry is the verbal equivalent of the action.

> The tree branglis[5] bosting[6] to the fall,
> With top trymbling, and branchis schakand all,
> Quhill finalie it get the lattir straik,
> Than, with ane rair doun duschis[7] the mekle aik,
> And with his faird[8] brekis doun bewis about.

The poetry not only imitates the sounds

> The souchand bir quisland amang the granis,[9]

it also conveys (in the second of these similes) the mass and strength of the oak resistant to the force of the wind, a sense of its bodily reality and steadfast firmness of character in its grim wrestling.

> And, natheles, the ilk tre, fixit fast,
> Stikkis to the rochis, nocht doun bet with the blast;
> For quhy? als far as his crop hych on breid[10]
> Strekis in the air, als far his ruite doith spreid
> Deip ondir erth, towart the hell adoun.

---

[1] plough.   [2] overthrown.   [3] prows.   [4] wave, breaker.
[5] brandishes.   [6] threatening.   [7] strikes.   [8] force, weight.
[9] branches.   [10] widely.

Like Ygdrasil, its roots go deeper than earth.

The similes throughout the *Aeneid* are the means by which
Virgil brings his own rural Italy into his heroic epic; they are
also the means by which Douglas brings in his own rural
Scotland. In these similes, he associates with the Henryson of
the *Fables* and the other medieval fabulists, as a poet of birds,
beasts and insects. The poetry responds delicately to the life
of the bird in the simile of the dove in Book V, subtly appre-
hends the changing movements of its flight from startled departure to smooth, balanced descent.

> Furth of hir hole, and rycht darn wynning[1] wane,[1]
> Quhair hir sweit nest is holkit[2] in the stane,
> So ferslie in the feildis furth scho springis,
> Quhill of hir fard[3] the hous riging ringis,
> And sone eftir, scherand the lownit[4] air,
> Doun from the hycht discendis soft and fair,
> Not besy wingit, bot planand esely.

The bird has a domestic life, too; its nest is 'sweit', though
'holkit in the stane', like a countryman's cottage in a barren
stony place. The simile of the ants in Book IV.

> Quhen thai depulye[5] the meikle bing of quheit . . .
> The blak swarm our the feildis walkis yarn,
> Tursand throw the gers thar pray to hiddillis[6] dern

is another instance of translation that has become Scottish
poetry made out of the poet's interest in directly observed
facts of his own countryside. So it is again with the simile of
the bees (Books I and VI); Douglas in his Scotland can share
with Virgil in his Italy a common pleasure in the brightness
and colours, the sweet tastes and smells, which make up the
summer life and activity of the bees.

> The huny smellis of the sweit tyme swid.

Douglas' version of the adder in Book II is close to experience
of the seemingly inert but suddenly dangerous, armed creature
confronting one on the moors when least expected.

[1] dwelling place	[2] hollowed out.	[3] force, motion.
[4] tranquil.	[5] spoil.	[6] hiding place.

> Hich up her nek strekand forgane the sone,
> With forkit tong intil hir mouth quitterand.

'I am inclined to think that Douglas gets more poetry out of Virgil than any other translator,' said Pound. If we turn from Douglas' treatment of the everyday world of directly observed facts to his treatment of some of the mythology in the *Aeneid* we find that here, too, he can be re-creative. His medieval moral and religious allegorical imagination in particular alters his vision and treatment. The Hous of Fame (Book IV) is rendered with all his medieval sense of Fame as a monstrosity, a huge hovering presence, an Aeschylean power over human affairs.

> By nycht scho fleis amyd the hevin throw out,
> Circuland the schaddow of the erd about . . .
> All day scho sittis, wacheand besely,
> Apon the top of nobillis housis to spy,
> Or on thir princis palice with towris hie,
> And with hir noyis gret ceteis affrais sche.[1]

Douglas would almost certainly have known Chaucer's *Hous of Fame* and, probably, the passage in Ovid's *Metamorphoses*; and there are the references in Chaucer to gossip, particularly Criseyde's fear of the gossiping tongues of medieval town or court that work mischief. But Douglas' concern is more Langlandian, more seriously moral and religious—'Fame is mischeif'. Similarly Douglas' version of Mercury descending (Book IV) brings out, with an added force, a new edge, the association of Mercury with Death.

> The paill sawlis he cachis furth of hell . . .
> And revis fra othir all sleip, and to the deid
> Closis thar ene . . .

[1] Cf. Prologue to Book 7:

> Hornit Hebawde, quhilk clepe we the nycht owle,
> Within hir caverne hard I schout and yowle;
> Laithlie of forme, wyth crukit camschow* beik,
> Vgsum to heir was hir wyld elriche screik:
> The wyld geis claking eik by nychtis tyde
> Attoure the citie fleand hard I glyde.
>   * twisted.

194

The mountain and the god, Atlas (Book IV), is in Douglas not only a Scottish mountain in winter but an image or figure of Age and Winter, as Saturn is in Henryson's *Testament of Cresseid.*

> His schulderis heildit[1] with new fallin snaw;
> Furth of the chyn of this ilk hassart[2] ald
> Gret fludis ischis, and stif ische schoklis cauld
> Doun from his sterne and grisly berd hingis.

The description of Etna has everything in common with the underworld experiences of Book IV. It parallels the description of Charybdis (which it follows in Book III) as a monstrous perturbation in nature, a demonic disturbance in the frame and order of things. In Douglas' version the medieval Hell— the Devil's 'smiddy'—is again a smoky, thunderous, acrid presence. Much of the material brought over by Virgil from the *Odyssy* must have seemed familiar to Douglas from the medieval romances and traditional tales. The Greek left behind in the land of the Cyclopes whose beard has grown long and who feeds on berries and roots would at once be recognizable to Douglas as the 'wild man of the woods'.

> A lenar wycht, na mair pynit, I ne saw.

The Cave of the Winds (Book I) has in Douglas' rendering again a thickly atmospheric 'Gothic' quality.

> Till Eolus cuntre, that wyndy regioun,
> Ane brudy[3] land . . .
> In gowstie cavis, the wyndis lowde quhisling . . .
> Beir with thair byr[4] the skyis, and drive about
> Erd, air, and se, quhenevir thai list blaw out.
> Thus the hie fadir almychtie in cavis dirk
> Thir wyndis hid for dreid sic wrangis thai wirk,
> And thar abuife sett wechty hillis huge.

'In gowstie cavis' renders Virgil's 'antro vasto' (Dryden has 'spacious cave'). This northern poetry, as it has become, brings out the ghostly sounds and character of the winds, turbulent wilful powers imprisoned under the earth and, lest

---

[1] covered.   [2] dotard, grey-head.   [3] broody.   [4] force.

they break out wholly and bring back chaos, curbed and controlled by a king placed in authority over them by the wise ruler of the universe—'the hie fadir almychtie'—the Virgilian conception again modified by Douglas' Christianity. The passage in Douglas' version has become something of a metaphor not only of the unruliness of nature and of men in his native Scotland, not only of the contemporary condition of the kingdom of Scotland, but of the soul of man. (Dryden's version, on the other hand, becomes a rhetorical expression of his royalist politics, Eolus an absolute monarch ruling by divine right in an age of popular revolutions and rebellions.

> With power imperial curbs the struggling winds . . .
> High in the hall the undaunted monarch sits.

The tone is that of panegyric. Dryden's concern is for public order, settled government, stability in the state—rather than for the soul.

Finally, there are the passages about old age which we may feel to have become very much Douglas himself speaking to us on the subject of growing old (as we may feel also about some of the passages in the *Canterbury Tales* and the opening of Henryson's *Testament of Cresseid* that they are especially personal) even though the speaker—Entellus, for example, the ageing champion in Book V—is a *dramatis persona* in a translated poem.

> Bot certanlie the dasyt bluid, now on dayis
> Walxis dolf[1] and dull throw myne unweildy age;
> The cald body has menist[2] my curage.
> Bot war I now, as umquhile[3] it hes bene,
> Ying as yone wanton woustour,[4] sa strang thai wene,
> Ya, had I now sic youthheid, traistis me . . .

There are parallel passages in Shakespeare. Douglas could associate the wrestling match between Entellus and Dares with the customs and traditions of his own country, the village wrestlings and the traditional contest between youth and age.

[1] faint.   [2] diminished.
[3] formerly.   [4] boaster.

> Lychtar on fuit and agil was the tane,
> And in his lusty youth sum deill ensuris;
> The tother of lymmis biggar and cors mair stur[1] is,
> Bot his faynt schankis gan for eild schaik.

When the young man has been defeated—by a strength that has proved to be greater than his own—Aeneas thus addresses him in words that, in Douglas' version, have assumed a Christian significance.

> Unsilly wycht! quhow did thi mynd invaid
> Sic gret wodnes! felis thow nocht yit, quod he,
> Othir strenth or mannis force has delt with the?
> Seis thow nocht weill thi self that thow art fey?
> Thairfor to God thow yeld the and obey.

Yet his words are, one feels, at the same time addressed by Douglas to himself. They express a personal wisdom—and a universal human wisdom. The centuries between seem to have fallen away. We seem to come very near to Douglas the man— 'a man speaking to men'.

[1] strong.

Note. The quotations are from John Small's edition of 1874 based on the printed text of 1553. There has now come out a S.T.S. edition based on a MS in the library of Trinity College, Cambridge.

16

Tradition and Robert Fergusson (1952)

What it means to belong in a tradition—the differences there may be between the productions of the same poet in two traditions—could not be more clearly illustrated than by the contrast between Fergusson's English and his Scots poems. In Scots Fergusson is a poet; in English he fails to be so. The explanation must be the obvious one, that in English Fergusson was trying to compose in a tradition to which he could not really belong. The choice between the two traditions presented itself to him, no doubt, as a choice between the two languages. Scots was Fergusson's 'real' language, the language which was more intimately a part of his personal life, the spoken language of that Scottish community to which he belonged. In the alien language which English remained[1] to him—inseparable from an alien tradition—he was capable only of superficial exercises.

It will not do for Scottish patriots to blame David Hume for, on the contrary, choosing English as his instrument. Considering the nature of Hume's philosophic speculations he could scarcely, in the eighteenth century, have done otherwise, unless he had chosen French. Had he lived in the time of Henryson or Dunbar he would, as inevitably, have composed in Latin. The realm of speculative thought was Hume's country, and he very justly takes his celebrated place in the history of European thought. But poetry is more intimately related to

[1] We may contrast Conrad, who seems to have been drawn to his adopted language by some powerful sympathy.

flesh and blood, and necessarily implies a community not of abstract entities but of flesh-and-blood people living together in a particular locality. Poetry implies such a community even when—as some poetry does—it implies a solitary individual's consciousness of his isolation from such a community.

Fergusson is not a solitary genius. His Scots poetry not only implies a Scottish community but is substantially communal. How otherwise explain the instant maturity of Fergusson's Scots poetry than by assuming an exceptional measure of co-operation between the poet and his community? There was clearly a living tradition of verse practice in Scots and there was also a custom of familiar verse communication in Scots. Almost from the moment when he began to compose in Scots, Fergusson—as happens with Burns also—is a mature poet.

We must, of course, distinguish the Scots verse of Fergusson and Burns from the folk ballads. They are not anonymous and impersonal; they are conscious poets moving with a considerable creative freedom of observation, less immersed in their conventions than the ballad-makers. Nevertheless, they are as Scots poets more completely at one with their community— their poetry more fully the product of a co-operation between themselves and their community—than the poetry we mostly read in books.[1]

Robert Fergusson belonged to the old Scottish community there still was in Edinburgh. Edinburgh was not yet, I think, a typically eighteenth-century city, though there was already an eighteenth-century 'polite' circle. David Hume belonged to it, and so did other distinguished personalities. It was 'polite' in the eighteenth-century sense, as the word was used of those who considered themselves to be the contemporary representatives of absolute civilization. The polite circle in Edinburgh must necessarily have been somewhat exclusive, but it was sustained by a consciousness that it was a Northern

[1] In this respect Fergusson is almost at the opposite extreme from modern authors such as Eliot or Conrad or James or Lawrence, who are essentially isolated, not simply ill at ease in modern society but conscious that there is no modern society which they can completely belong to.

counterpart of the greater 'polite' societies in London and Paris, the metropolitan centres of European culture.

For European culture was by the eighteenth century becoming more and more metropolitan—metropolitan and exclusive. Up to about the seventeenth century the culture of Europe had lived and found creative expression in a widespread variety of small local communities, in various dialects and at various social levels. It had ranged from the popular to the sophisticated, often combining both in one and the same form of art or poetry or drama. It appears to have been in the cities of Italy about the time of the Renaissance that societies of the cultivated began deliberately to separate themselves from the rustic life of the countryside round about. Elizabethan London—Shakespeare's London—was still, on the whole, unaffected by the Italian example. Fergusson's Edinburgh was more like Elizabethan London than an eighteenth-century city. Fergusson's Edinburgh, judging by his Scots poetry, was one of the local centres of resistance in Europe to the hardening urbanization and centralization of European culture. Of course, the whole situation forced a separation of Scots poetry from the rest of the poetry of Europe and from what Arnold called 'the best that is known and thought in the world', in the great world, the 'current of ideas' circulating in the metropolitan centres of Europe. Fergusson's poetry, and that of Burns, are by comparison with Henryson's and Dunbar's less varied, more locally limited, in their interests. That was no fault of Fergusson and Burns but of changes taking place throughout Europe as a whole—the changes which have brought about the modern world. The Scots poetry of Fergusson and Burns no doubt suffered from its isolation—an isolation it had itself vigorously to maintain, or perish; but there is equally no doubt that the culture of Europe as a whole was impoverished by the exclusion of various local cultures and their consequent gradual withering. What might have continued to nourish and enrich the culture of Europe as a whole was allowed gradually to be lost to it.

Fergusson as a composer of verses in English may even be

said to have in that respect belonged to the Edinburgh polite circle. But as a Scots poet he did not belong to it. As a Scots poet he belonged to an Edinburgh which was still—despite the presence in it of that polite circle reflecting the rays of eighteenth-century rational enlightenment—thoroughly rural in character and speech, the town focus of a wider agricultural community.

The old Scottish organic community of the Edinburgh of Fergusson's poems was typical of the older communities which have been destroyed by the industrialization of the mechanical era. It was really very old indeed: it had its roots deep in the past.

The relation of Fergusson's poetry to dance and drama is not simply one of historical descent. It is immediately related to the contemporary folk festivals, fairs and rustic holidays which still expressed and renewed the essential jollity of a peasant folk, in accord with the seasonal rhythms. This, it seems to me, is the explanation of why the poetry of Fergusson, and of Burns after him, is essentially bucolic and bacchanalian in character. Even those poems of Fergusson which do not specifically describe and celebrate feasts, fairs and holidays still carry in their rhythm the original impulse of the dance.

One or two of Fergusson's poems are in the traditional flyting or humorously abusive manner. Fergusson's best poem in the flyting manner is, I think, his address *To the Tron-kirk Bell*. The speaker's exasperation (in this dramatic monologue) with the jarring bell is itself part of the comedy. There are thus two comic characters, the exasperated speaker and his antagonist, the fiendish bell, which—in the extremity of his exasperation —he threatens:

> Wanwordy, crazy, dinsome thing,
> As e'er was fram'd to jow or ring,
> What gar'd them sic in steeple hing
> > They ken themsel',
> But weel wat I they coudna bring
> > War sounds frae hell.
> What de'il are ye? that I shud ban,
> Your neither kin to pat nor pan;

> Nor *uly pig*, nor *master-cann*
>   But weel may gie
> Mair pleasure to the ear o' man
>   Than stroak o' thee.
>
> .   .   .   .   .
>
> O! war I provost o' the town,
> I swear by a' the pow'rs aboon,
> I'd bring ye wi' a reesle down;
>   Nor shud you think
> (Sae sair I'd crack and clour your crown)
>   Again to clink.
>
> For whan I've toom'd the muckle cap,
> An' fain wud fa' owr in a nap,
> Troth I cud doze as sound's a tap,
>   Wer't na for thee,
> That gies the tither weary chap
>   To waukin me.
>
> I dreamt ae night I saw Auld Nick;
> Quo he, 'this bell o' mine's a trick,
> A wylie piece o' politic,
>   A cunnin snare
> To trap fock in a cloven stick,
>   'Ere they're aware.'

What account should be taken of Calvinism in relation to Fergusson's poetry? Calvinism was, after all, the successor in Scotland of medieval Catholicism. Although it emerges from the split in the Church, which we call the Reformation, it is itself a development of an element in the Catholicism which it opposes, rather than an entirely new thing. In spite of the fanaticism of Calvinists, Calvinist theology is rigorously logical, indeed materialistic and mechanical in character. I believe that in many people Calvinism became the religious counter part—the reverse side, if you like—of the New Science and of the rationalistic enlightenment which in other minds became scepticism. Calvinism appears to have had its strongest hold on the thriving tradespeople of the town; and it evidently fitted in with the change from the traditional agricultural order to mechanical industrialism. Calvinism is therefore one of the forces *external* to the poetry of Fergusson and Burns.

Because it is not an element in the organic community it is not an element in that poetry. Calvinistic characters—such as Burns's Holy Willie—do indeed appear in the poetry, but as *objects* pointed at by satire. From this point of view these characters are hypocritical, aspiring—or pretending—to be superior to natural instincts; they have lost the traditional wisdom, the shrewd self-knowledge and knowledge of human nature and of the conditions of human life, possessed by the members of the organic community. But even as objects of satire Calvinistic characters or attitudes scarcely appear in Fergusson's poetry; so that one wonders if it was not nineteenth-century Scotland rather than eighteenth-century Scotland which was more soaked in Calvinism. Perhaps Fergusson's poetry expresses only one side of eighteenth-century Scottish life, but if so it was the traditional side that persisted despite Calvinism on the one hand and the 'enlightenment' on the other.

Fergusson's *Elegy on John Hogg, Late Porter to the University of St Andrews* is a poem in the Scots tradition of humorous elegy. Here in the concreteness of a character and in dialogue, it is not too much to say that we have dramatized the clash between Calvinist Presbyterianism represented by John Hogg and eighteenth-century enlightenment represented by the students. For John is a man of the Bible which, as he understands it, sanctions him in a sound common-sense belief in the solidity and stability of this earth. John's religion is combined with careful looking after the pence. Poverty he regards as immoral. (We find the same conjunction typified by the Puritan father and the members of his sect in Crabbe's masterly tale, *The Frank Courtship*.) So John thrives in a worldly sense, as he feels morally bound to do, and, though a college porter, leaves behind him at his death a handsome estate:

> 'I hae nae meikle skill,' quo' he,
> 'In what you ca' philosophy;
> It tells that baith the earth and sea
>   Rin round about;
> Either the Bible tells a lie,
>   Or you're a' out.

203

'It's i' the *psalms* o' DAVID writ,
That this wide warld ne'er shou'd flit,
But on the waters coshly sit
    Fu' steeve and lasting;
An' was na he a head o' wit
    At sic contesting!

.   .   .   .   .

'Ye ken what ails maun ay befal
The chiel that will be prodigal;
When wasted to the very spaul
    He turns his tusk,
For want o' comfort to his saul
    O' hungry husk.'

Ye royit lowns! just do as he'd do;
For mony braw green SHAW and MEADOW
He's left to cheer his dowy widow,
    His winsome *Kate*,
That to him prov'd a canny she-dow,
    Baith ear' and late.

The poet's identity is scarcely threatened by John; the effect is more humorous than satiric. But a deadlier threat to the traditional life was about to develop. To appreciate the full effect of the changes that brought about the dissolution of the organic community, we might well contrast the Edinburgh of Fergusson's poetry with Coketown in *Hard Times* or with one of D. H. Lawrence's impressions of the industrial towns, for example Wiggiston in *The Rainbow*.[1]

> Everything was amorphous, yet everything repeated itself endlessly.
> . . . The place had the strange desolation of a ruin. Colliers hanging about in gangs and groups, or passing along the asphalt pavements heavily to work, seemed not like living people, but like spectres. The rigidity of the blank streets, the homogeneous amorphous sterility of the whole suggested death rather than life. There was no meeting-place, no centre, no artery, no organic formation.

With Wiggiston, there could be no greater contrast than the

[1] Cf. 'Nottingham and the Mining Countryside' in *Phoenix*.

Edinburgh of Fergusson's poetry. It is therefore perhaps not the least value which that poetry might have for us that it makes possible such a contrast, that it keeps alive—even in the modern waste land—the recognition of some of the possibilities of life.

For, concretely present in Fergusson's Scots poetry, vivid to our sense, presented without idealization but with Hogarthian realism so that all its faults are sharply distinct, is Fergusson's Edinburgh. It becomes almost as familiar to us, while we read, as if we ourselves were living in it. Here is how the Scottish folk talked, how they lived; here is communicated their conviviality, their jollity and their humour. We listen to their very accents; we enter into the very rhythm of their actions. Fergusson does not simply describe the Edinburgh life—he does describe it with vividness—but his poetry is itself that life, its expression and embodiment.

> *Auld Reikie!* thou'rt the canty hole,
> A bield for mony a caldrife soul,
> Wha snugly at thine ingle loll,
> > Baith warm and couth;
> While round they gar the bicker roll
> > To weet their mouth.

> When merry *Yule-day* comes, I trow
> You'll scantlins find a hungry mou;
> Sma' are our cares, our stamacks fou
> > O' gusty gear,
> And kickshaws, strangers to our view,
> > Sin Fairn-year.

> .   .   .   .   .

> Then, tho' at odds wi' a' the warl',
> Amang oursells we'll never quarrel;
> Tho' Discord gie a canker'd snarl
> > To spoil our glee,
> As lang's there's pith into the barrel
> > We'll drink and 'gree.

> *Fidlers,* your pins in temper fix,
> And roset weel your fiddle-sticks,

But banish vile Italian tricks
           From out your quorum:
Nor *fortes* wi' *pianos* mix,
           Gie's *Tulloch Gorum.*

For nought can cheer the heart sae weil
As can a canty Highland reel,
It even vivifies the heel
           To skip and dance:
Lifeless is he wha canna feel
           Its influence.[1]

[1] These stanzas are from a poem called *The Daft-Days.* The 'daft days' are the days of Yule and Hogmanay. The poem begins with an impression of the December bleakness of the surrounding country and the blear-eyed sun. But Auld Reikie is built to keep out the winter. Convivial companies are gathered where there is light and warmth and a plentiful outpouring of food and drink from the winter stores. The influence of Horace is discernible in the poem.

17

Burns's 'To a Louse' and 'Holy Willie's Prayer' (1956)

To a Louse and *Holy Willie's Prayer*, are virtually dramatic monologues, though in the first the poet himself is the character speaking or has assumed this role. The opening of *To a Louse* is dramatically sudden:

> Ha! where ye gaun, ye crawlin ferlie!
> Your impudence protects you sairly:
> I canna say but ye strunt rarely,
>   Owre gauze and lace;
> Tho', faith, I fear ye dine but sparely
>   On sic a place.

The manner is that of 'flyting', yet it is clear that abuse is mingled with admiration for the amazing agility and strut of the creature. The poet cannot help having a certain sympathy even with a louse, which like 'mice and men' also 'maun live'. Gauze and lace are very fine but not edible. They are no more use to the louse than was the jewel on the dunghill to the cock of the fable. But the impudence of the louse rouses the poet's indignant fury:

> Ye ugly, creepin', blastit wonner,
> Detested, shunn'd, by saunt an' sinner,
> How dare ye set your fit upon her,
>   Sae fine a lady!
> Gae somewhere else, and seek your dinner
>   On some poor body.

The comic poetic imagination magnifies and multiplies the diminutive creature into whole populations of its kind all in a state of vigorous animation, whole nations in a beggar's rags:

> Swith, in some beggar's haffet squattle;
> There ye may creep, and sprawl, and sprattle
> Wi' ither kindred, jumping cattle,
>   In shoals and nations;
> Whare horn nor bane ne'er dare unsettle
>   Your thick plantations.

In the development of this poem the shifts of attention and sudden excitements of the observer are reproduced in his speaking voice and correspond dramatically to the movements and struggling upward progression of the indefatigable, intrepid creature till it reaches the summit of Jenny's new bonnet:

> Na, faith ye yet! ye'll no be right
>   Till ye've got on it,
> The vera tapmost, tow'ring height
>   O' Miss's bonnet.

The observer is curious to see how far it will get until it overtops the summit of pride.

At this point in the poem there is a shift of attention to Jenny herself. The irony is that no doubt she thinks she is making a grand impression in church in her new bonnet and Sunday finery, unaware of the indignity being imposed on her by the louse. The old traditional feeling about 'pride and vanity' is here again in the impression of Jenny giving herself airs, proud Jenny:

> O, Jenny, dinna toss your head,
> An' set your beauties a' abread!
> Ye little ken what cursed speed
>   The blastie's makin'!

The poem is both a comedy—based on the incongruity of louse and fine lady—and a moral fable:

> O wad some Pow'r the giftie gie us
> To see oursels as others see us!

208

Holy Willie's Prayer, perhaps the finest of Burns's satiric poems, is a dramatic monologue in which the mounting fervency of Willie's eloquence, as he himself is more and more carried away by it, is itself comic, an aspect of the whole grand effect of ironic comedy. The irony is that in his eloquent outpouring Willie completely exposes his own nature and instincts without exposing himself to himself, without disturbing his own inordinate self-conceit. The poem is thus, among other things, a study in unconscious hypocrisy. Willie kneels at the centre of his little parochial world, so vividly present in the imagery, in direct relation with his God—and what a God! The poem's implied criticism of the character of Holy Willie is at the same time a criticism of the Calvinism that shaped the character; they stand and fall together. Holy Willie's is a God who pleases himself and, in doing so, damns ten times the number of people he saves, all for his glory:

> O Thou, wha in the Heavens dost dwell,
> Wha, as it pleases best thysel',
> Sends ane to heaven and ten to hell,
>   A' for thy glory,
> And no for ony guid or ill
>   They've done afore thee!
>
> I bless and praise thy matchless might,
> When thousands thou hast left in night,
> That I am here afore thy sight,
>   For gifts an' grace,
> A burnin' an' a shinin' light
>   To a' this place.

Salvation has no relation to one's moral conduct, but depends on 'election'—and Willie has no doubt that he is one of the elect. It is a damning criticism of Willie that he can 'bless and praise' a God thus conceived. But Willie is sublimely unconscious of the figure he cuts. His arrogance is so unbounded as to amount to caricature. While thousands are lost in darkness (such is his vision of mankind), Willie is 'a burnin' an' a shinin' light'. His 'humility' is a form of pride:

> What was I, or my generation,
> That I should get sic exaltation?
> I, wha deserve sic just damnation
>   For broken laws. . . .

The laws were not broken by Willie, but before he was born:

> Five thousand years 'fore my creation,
>   Thro' Adam's cause.

Thus even Willie's faults are not his responsibility but are part of the divine plan for his benefit, since he is 'chosen'.

> When frae my mither's womb I fell,
> Thou might hae plunged me in hell,
> To gnash my gums, to weep and wail
>   In burnin' lake,
> Where damned devils roar an' yell,
>   Chain'd to a stake.

Though the idiom throughout the poem is of course 'comic', the imagery that Willie conceives here is as inhuman, as unnatural as Lady Macbeth's when she is doing violence to her own nature as a woman, and it reveals how far the Calvinist Holy Willie has deviated from nature and sense. Yet, even at this point he can rise to a sublimity of complacent self-satisfaction:

> Yet I am here a chosen sample,
> To show thy grace is great and ample;
> I'm here a pillar in thy temple,
>   Strong as a rock;
> A guide, a buckler, an example
>   To a' thy flock.

God's grace excludes the greater part of mankind, but so long as it includes Willie it is 'great and ample'.

Willie goes on to reveal in what respects he is 'an example'. He speaks of his own sins of the flesh as if they were ills of the flesh, afflictions sent to him which he must bear. After declaring, and apparently believing, that he is not as other men who drink, swear, sing, and dance, the opposite begins to come out —and that he is in his way a lusty fellow:

> But yet, O Lord! confess I must,
> At times I'm fash'd wi' fleshy lust.

He excuses himself for one of his lapses by saying that that night he 'was fou'. After what he had just said about his immunity from the local drinking habits, we thus learn incidentally that there are occasions when he is not so. But his sins are of course not Willie's personal affair, not his responsibility; they are inflicted on him, sent to save him from pride.

> Maybe thou lets this fleshy thorn
> Beset thy servant e'en and morn,
> Lest he owre high and proud should turn
>   'Cause he's sae gifted.

Willie remains unshakably convinced of his own exceptional merits, and thus continues to exemplify the pride that he presumes himself to be saved from.

The 'prayer', as it goes on, reveals a Holy Willie full of most un-Christian feelings towards his neighbours, full of envy, malice, and all uncharitableness, particularly towards those among them who have in some way offended Willie himself and the small band of the 'chosen'. A fierce energy, a ferocity of personal vindictiveness and spite kindles the eloquence of his prayer against them. His concern is that they should *not* be spared, that they should get their deserts:

> Lord, mind Gaun Hamilton's deserts,
> He drinks, an' swears, and plays at cartes . . .
> An' whan we chasten'd him therefore,
> Thou kens how he bred sic a splore,
> As set the warld in a roar
>   O' laughin' at us;
> Curse thou his basket and his store,
>   Kail and potatoes.

The world that laughs—a laughter not to be borne—is Willie's own small parochial world, the world of his neighbour's 'basket and store, kail and potatoes'. The God of all mankind is called upon fervently, in Old Testament phraseology, to curse Gaun Hamilton's basket, store, kail and potatoes, and

also to curse the Presbytery of Ayr. The comic satiric effect
depends on the disproportion:

> Thy strong right hand, Lord, make it bare
> Upo' their heads;
> Lord, weigh it down, and dinna spare.

Willie's God might here be the village schoolmaster.

With the repetitions of 'dinna spare' and of 'Lord' (as,
earlier, of 'chosen') Willie's eloquence rises to a climax, which
is sublime in manner but comic in effect:

> But, for thy people's sake, destroy 'em,
> And dinna spare.

He sees his neighbours as the Philistines of the Old Testament,
the enemies of God's chosen. The mercies which at the same
time Willie asks for himself are both 'temp'ral and divine',
both 'gear and grace'. It is clear that for Willie the increase of
temporal blessings, the multiplication of earthly goods ('gear'),
is the way the divine grace favours the chosen. Worldly pros-
perity is the visible and outward sign and effect of the divine
grace. Willie expects to have it both ways, to prosper both in
a material and a spiritual sense.

18

Burn's Epistles in Relation to Eighteenth-century Verse (1958)

Burns's verse Epistles offer, among other things, an opportunity to re-examine the distinction between eighteenth-century Scots and English poetry. Imitation of the Satires and Epistles of Horace and Juvenal was one of the established modes of the English Augustan verse. Some of the greatest poetry of Pope, notably his *Moral Essays*, is an extension or development of that mode. After Pope, there are Johnson's imitations of Juvenal, his *London* and *The Vanity of Human Wishes*. Burns, on the other hand, carries on not from Pope but from Fergusson and Ramsay, his immediate predecessors in Scots. But Ramsay was an imitator of Horace, in Scots. Here, then, seems to be some common ground for a comparison between eighteenth-century Scots and English poetry.

If we try to view Burns' Epistles as an extension of the Horatian mode in Scots we have to consider what has happened to Horace. I do not mean that Burns read Horace and deliberately imitated him. I am referring to something that was already a presence in Scots verse tradition as it came to Burns from Ramsay. What was there in the life and manners of the rural, market-town communities of eighteenth-century Scotland that could associate in Scots verse with Horace? There is the urbane side of Horace; but there is also his homely side—the homely traditional wisdom he inherited from his

213

father and his rustic forebears. Broadly speaking, it was this homely side that might associate with Scots; whereas it was the urbane side that on the whole appealed to the English Augustans.

Being a member of an urbane, a metropolitan polite society, Pope could compose his Imitations in the full consciousness of a contemporary European civilization in which Roman Augustan models counted—models of poetry, of morals and of humane living. He could feel, or imagine, that there was some equivalence between his English Augustan order and the Roman one; that ancient and modern together formed a single inclusive European order. He could feel that he and the Roman poet were associates in absolute civilization, as if they were contemporaries.

Pope could, of course, clearly perceive that the society around him in the England of Queen Anne was un-ideal. He would not otherwise have been a satirist. But it was because he could reach out to an ideal society beyond the society in which he lived that he could perceive the un-ideality so clearly. Though he did not share the prevalent complacency, he was at the same time sustained by a confidence that something of the ideal had been realized, was indeed impressively present in the society of his Queen Anne England. Furthermore, Pope's ideal of society had been provided for him not simply by the Roman model, but by the great religious tradition of Europe. The greatest of the English Augustans, Pope was also the last in the line from Donne, the line of the poetry of *metaphysical* wit. He transcends his Augustan age as in the fullest sense an *imaginative* poet.

Burns, on the other hand, has no feeling for, no reaching out towards, any ideal society. No such apprehension, or illusion, made it possible for him to detach himself in spirit from the society in which he worked, ate, drank, conversed, and was convivial. Only at moments of reckless disregard or defiance does he feel liberated from the forms and conventions of his society. At these moments the barriers are broken down between man and man, and a warm sense of a common humanity prevails. It is in this sense of a common humanity that Burns discovers his positive strength. At its clearest it becomes regard for intrinsic human worth independent of wealth and rank, and of social and moral forms and conventions.

Friendship matters to Burns as to Horace. (Love matters more than it does to Horace. But in Burns' Epistles it is friendship that is expressed.) Burns' Epistles are his part in the familiar exchanges between man and man, the genial witty intimacies that passed between him and his friends and fellow poets. Casually, informally, freely, as in an uninhibited conversational flow, he ranges over the interests and concerns of the passing hours, the moods and attitudes changing easily the one into the other in a poetry of unusual flexibility. I think we must acknowledge that Burns' Epistles are neither so profound nor comprehensive, as criticism of man and society, as are the four epistles of Pope's *Moral Essays* in which Pope's profoundly serious concern for civilization is inseparable from his concern for a human centrality. Nor do they combine a dignified formality, a poetic 'decorum', with colloquial ease and witty play of intelligence as do Pope's Epistles.

This brings me to what is perhaps the most obvious and at the same time essential difference between Burns and the English Augustans, the absence in Burns of regard for the value which they called 'politeness'—their particular ideal of civilized human living of which formal manners were the outward or public expression. We find in Burns not simply a disregard for 'decorum' but at times a reckless defiance of it, a defiance of propriety, of correctness, of 'good form' in social and moral behaviour that had its equivalent in the formal regularity of the couplet verse. In this, Burns is much more like the Byron of the *Vision of Judgment* and *Don Juan* than he is like Pope. Recklessness can hardly be said to have been the note of Horace either, Horace who believed in playing safe and taking the pleasures of the hour moderately. The recklessness of Burns (as of Byron) goes together with the air of casual improvization and spontaneous flow.

> Sae I've begun to scrawl, but whether
> In rhyme or prose, or baith tegither,
> Or some hotch-potch that's rightly neither . . .
>
> (2nd Epistle to Lapraik.)

And it goes together with the extravagances of the rhyming.

> Rivin the words to gar them clink.
>
> (2nd Epistle to Davies.)

Overflow of spontaneous geniality and generous sympathies, warmth of friendship and love, warm-heartedness, kindliness —these are the values celebrated in this side of Burns' poetry.

For Pope, to be natural was to be sensible; the head was as important as the heart. Burns, too, has *his* kind of good sense. But it has nothing to do with 'decorum' or 'polite' learning. Thus in the first Epistle to Lapraik he expresses humorous contempt for the pedantic book-learning of school and college, and his reliance on what he calls 'honest nature' and 'countra wit'. But, though it has nothing to do with 'decorum' or 'polite learning', Burns' kind of good sense or humorous shrewdness is also traditional—the traditional wisdom of the Scottish country people. It is absent from Byron, who is too much of the Regency to have it. But it is pervasive in Burns' flowing poetry as a steadying element or ballast. It is a traditional wisdom present in his Scots colloquial idiom itself, the residue or product of centuries of hard experience and struggle of an impoverished country people. This is the equivalent in Burns of Horace's homely wisdom, his paternal inheritance. The flights and diversions of high spirits and genial witty fancies in the poetry are continually brought up hard against recognition of un-genial facts, the facts of the human condition aggravated in a poor country—toil, struggle, poverty, hunger, old age, and death. The life of poverty in the country is not conceived as a chosen way of life, not a retirement into the simple pleasures of the country when jaded with the city pleasures of the rich, but a necessity to be borne till death. This is the dark, stubborn background to the *Carpe Diem* theme or note in Burns. The headlong course, the dash, the gay courage or bravado of the reckless human creature is checked,

216

controlled by this recurrent, humorous, self-deprecating recognition of the facts of existence against which one comes to grief in this 'wild warl''.

The reckless note, together with the classic Epicurean carelessness, is absent from the English Augustans—except in cautionary accounts of rakes' progresses as a characteristic of the rakes. Neither Pope nor Johnson could be reckless. Pope didn't need to be. The things he valued were sufficiently valued also, and to some extent realized, in his society in which, as a satiric poet, he had the recognized function to correct or refine. Johnson, though deeply disturbed by life, had to struggle against his gloomy broodings, his melancholia, with the whole strength and weight of his powerful intelligence and character. He had to '*make* the happiness he did not find'. He could not be light.

In much of the minor English poetry of the century, poetic or conventional diction, and poetic or conventional themes exclude other, more colloquial elements of language and other aspects of life, and therefore exclude a whole range of life. Elevation of style also, as in much of the eighteenth-century Miltonic verse, goes with moral elevation and tends to put the poet and therefore his readers into a false position. It promotes hypocrisy, one of the vices that Burns most hates. Characteristically, in Burns' poetry the homely colloquial Scots element in his vocabulary plays humorously and wittily against the conventional diction and phrases. The effect is a breaking-up of the poetic conventions and therefore of the moral and social conventions they imply. So in Burns' poetry the spontaneous life, the generous sympathies and, equally important, the humorous, witty, shrewd, traditional wisdom break through.

Burns' Epistles take their rise from conversation between friends, alehouse conversation—not coffee-house conversation —in village, or market-town. But in alehouse conversation, or conversation at convivial gatherings, the life of the whole bucolic community flowed together under Bacchanalian influence and came to a full bodily, rather than mental, consciousness. The genial spirits flow or overflow in 'social noise' (as Burns calls it). In the Epistles the flow of the talk is speeded up, goes as if to a fast dance-tune on a fiddle. The animation of country-fairs and dances animates the rhythms, kindling the wit and humorous fancies.

Poetry itself is one of the supreme values in life for Burns. (He is explicit about this in *Epistle to Smith*, and *first and second Epistle to Lapraik*, and *second Epistle to Davies*.) What he calls his 'rhyming' is itself identified with the genial flow of life, high spirits and generous sympathies. Poetry is for Burns spontaneous life rising unconstricted into the brightness of consciousness—

> That out of life's own self-delight had sprung
> The abounding glittering jet[1]

—a fine excess, a gay exuberance, an outflowing from the sources, the deep springs of being. It is itself its own justification and meaning.

> (For me an aim I never fash
> I rhyme for fun)

Poetry (as Burns opposes it to 'prose') is spontaneous life at its fullest, as opposed to living coldly by rule, to rationality, to worldliness, money-making, conventionality, the mathematical regulation and regimentation of life (*Epistle to Smith*).

> O ye douce folk that live by rule . . .

But of those like himself he says:

> Nae rules nor roads observin
> They zig-zag on.[2]

There is something of the inebriated vagabond. The sense of sharing in a common humanity promotes humility, an acknowledgment of common faults, frailties and failings. In the poetry of Burns—as in that of Catullus, Propertius, Villon— we discover ourselves and our faults. We discover other men who in their faults are like ourselves. And we discover a value in quintessential life, flowing in every man alike, independent of rank and wealth. The Muses are 'the ragged Nine'.

---

[1] Yeats' *Meditations in Time of Civil War*.
[2] Cp. 'inorganic logical straightness and not the crooked path of life' (Yeats).

19

Translation into Scots (1948)

Mr. Douglas Young's poems in *A Braird o Thristles* are mostly in Scots but wear an 'international' aspect which I should like to examine. Since the eighteenth century and in recent practice, Scots, dissociated from uses other than that of poetic composition, has begun to suffer the disabilities of poetic diction. It may be questioned if authentic poetry can come of a language which continues to be used only for poetic practice. (Equally, of course, a language in which poetry is no longer practised perishes from the top downwards.) Too often in reading contemporary poems in Scots one experiences the sensation of meeting something one has met before, something done over again, with literary accomplishment, after having been done in the Ballads, for example. For even when the poem is headed 'Til the Andantino frae Gluck's Orpheus', and some attempt is made to break away from the rhythms of the Ballads to reproduce the grand operatic manner of the eighteenth century, the phrases are still the familiar ballad phrases.

> Delicatelie kaimit gowden hair
> sudna bind about my hairt sae sair.

We have met the 'kaimit gowden hair' and the 'hairt sae sair' how many times before! It would be worth considering, perhaps, why such a large proportion of these 'international' poems are in popular ballad modes—some of which are a device for getting it both ways as Auden and his school-friends

219

once showed how (you laugh both with and at the people, or you share the primitive horror thrill while at the same time holding superiorly aloof). Mr. Young's Scots poems include translations from French, German, Russian, Lithuanian, Greek, Hebrew and Chinese. If Mr. Young's attitude to Scots resembles Joyce's curiously external attitude to words, he is at the same time an amateur of diverse languages and civilizations after the pattern of Pound. Pound was, like Joyce, an experimenter of genius. But his work does illustrate in some of its weaknesses one aspect of our modern trouble. So many diverse civilizations and cultures have flowed together that the one blurs the other, until no one of them is felt deeply any longer or realized distinctly. The question of how to make a right use of foreign influences—raised by Mr. Young's translations from here, there and everywhere—is therefore a very serious one for us all.

Scots never passed through the more recent phases of the European mind which English and French have passed through. For that reason, Mr. Young's *The Kirkyaird By The Sea*, a rendering of Valéry's *Le Cimetière marin*, may be regarded as one of the most daring experiments recently undertaken in Scots. For unless Scots can assimilate the phase of the mind to which Valéry and one or two European poets and novelists of the last generation belong, it cannot go on to achieve poetry. For poetry is always contemporary. It has its timeless aspect as it has its temporal aspect. But, in its temporal aspect, it is contemporary or nothing; it lives, if it lives at all, in relation to a particular time, and that particular time can be no other than the present. Before poetry in Scots can again be contemporary—before it can *be*—it must necessarily have passed through and a little beyond the most recent phase of the civilized consciousness.

Mr. Young's Scots version of *Le Cimetière marin* may be compared with Mr. Cecil Day Lewis's version in English, which is a good example of what is regarded as poetry in England and which many do not distinguish from the authentic modern poetry—Mr. Eliot's *Four Quartets*. Mr. Day Lewis has the advantage over Mr. Young of an English language that has had a Yeats and an Eliot, near-equivalents to a Valéry. On the other hand, Shelley's *Adonais* echoes rather too audibly through Mr. Day Lewis's version and represents an earlier phase of the English consciousness that Mr. Day Lewis has evidently never quite assimilated. Perhaps for the same reason, Mr. Day Lewis regularly dissolves the sharpness of the Yeats and Eliot phrases from which his own are derived. Mr. Day Lewis's poem is consequently a vague, if splendid appearing and sounding, rhetoric. His phrases leave the impression of having been subtle phrases, far subtler than Mr. Young's Scots, but when we examine them they are just on the point of dissolving away like dream complexities which seem so complex yet are at the same time so indistinct. Mr. Young's phrases, derived from the Ballads and from Dunbar and Henryson, are often closer to exact sensation and therefore to graspable thought, as in the excellent lines:

> But in thir nicht, wechtit wi marble stane,
> a drowie fowk doun at the tree-ruits lain
> hae sideit wi you in slaw solemnitie

> They hae dwyneit intil a thick nonentitie,
> the reid clay drank the whyte identitie,
> the gift o life has gane intil the fleurs.

But Mr. Young's poem is necessarily simpler than Valéry, Rilke, Yeats or Eliot. The exact definition, by means of exact verbal reproduction of sensation, of the subtle and complex thought and experience of the recent European consciousness is beyond Mr. Young's Scots. *The Kirkyaird By The Sea* is less a translation than a simplification, though it is less simple than other modern Scots poems. It may be, then, that a Scottish poet cannot penetrate the most living contemporary thought and experience by means of Scots but only by means of contemporary English as spoken by himself. The gap between his realizable experience and the Ballads or Dunbar or Henryson is too great.

Bibliography

MIDDLE SCOTS TEXTS

The Kingis Quair, edited by J. Mackay Mackenzie (Faber & Faber).

The Poems of Robert Henryson, edited by Harvey Wood (Oliver & Boyd).

The Poems of William Dunbar, edited by J. Mackay Mackenzie, and now (1961) revised by Bruce Dickins (Faber & Faber).

Gavin Douglas's *Aeneid:* John Small's edition of 1874 based on the printed text of 1553. A Scottish Texts Society edition based on a manuscript in Trinity College Library, Cambridge, has now been published.

David Lindsay's *Ane Satyre of the Thri Estaitis,* edited by J. Kinsley (Cassell, 1954).

There are editions of most of the older Scots poets by the Scottish Texts Society and the Saltire Society.

Index

227